RISK
INTELLIGENCE

RISK
INTELLIGENCE

Learning to Manage
What We Don't Know

David Apgar

HARVARD BUSINESS SCHOOL PRESS
BOSTON, MASSACHUSETTS

978-1-59139-954-4 (ISBN 13)

Library of Congress Cataloging-in-Publication Data

Apgar, David.
   Risk intelligence : learning to manage what we don't know / David Apgar.
      p. cm.
   Includes bibliographical references.
   ISBN 1-59139-954-8
1. Risk management.   I. Title.
   HD61.A64 2006
   658.15'5—dc22   2006002371

The paper used in this publication meets the minimum requirements of the American National Standard for Information Sciences—Permanence of Paper for Printed Library Materials, ANSI Z39.48-1992.

To Helen and Holt Apgar

CONTENTS

Acknowledgments   ix

1   Changing Your Approach to Risk   1

2   Separating Learnable Risks from Random Ones in
    Business Decisions   23

3   Scoring Your Risk Intelligence (or Risk IQ)   63

4   Conducting a Risk Strategy Audit   105

5   Building Networks That Can Adapt to Risk   143

6   Raising Your Risk Intelligence Systematically   183

Notes   199
Index   205
About the Author   211

ACKNOWLEDGMENTS

My first thanks go to the reader, who may be a little curious about how I came to write this book—a practical guide to making decisions about *nonfinancial* risks that throws a fair amount of *financial* risk management orthodoxy overboard. The answer is that I spent years on financial risk management—as a technically oriented investment banker for financial institutions at Lehman Brothers, as an adviser in the Treasury Department's bank supervisory arm, as a McKinsey consultant focused on money center and multilateral bank risk management, and as the manager of the Corporate Executive Board's best-practices program for insurers. The combination forced me to solve financial risk management problems from an unusually wide variety of angles.

About five years ago, however, I helped launch the first of several best-practices programs at the board for executives who have to deal with risk in nonfinancial sectors. Imagine my surprise when I found the best financial risk management theory and practice in the world really didn't address the needs of people running nonfinancial businesses. Financial risk management doesn't have to deal with the vast differences in what and how fast people can learn about *real* risks—about operating risks, and technology risks, and business risks, and security risks, and strategic risks. And yet the vast majority of texts and consultant presentations try to shoehorn these nonfinancial risks into the standard financial risk management framework. So I had to write this book.

My second thanks go to the hundreds of members of the Corporate Executive Board's programs for CFOs, treasurers, and controllers whose alert questions and probing discussions have shaped my view of existing best risk management practice. Unlike the board's studies, this book goes beyond demonstrated practice to what seems to be missing from the modern risk management toolbox. To be effective, such a book needs the firmest possible foundation of what people are actually doing, and for that I owe a great debt of gratitude to the board's creative and diligent members.

To these principal debts I would like to add some personal notes of thanks. Big thanks go to Stephen Altschul of the National Institutes of Health for his unstinting friendship, for providing a remarkable window onto how hard thinking about probability is shaping our view of genetics and evolution, and for orienting me to technical aspects of information theory that underlie some of the practical tools in this volume. In particular, he showed where the book's definition of *relevance* as the complement of the surprise, improbability, or information content of business experience subject to a risk intelligence score may fit into standard information theory.

Joe Firestone, who runs Knowledge Management Consortium International, provided patient counsel and useful argument. His painstaking review of the manuscript improved it immeasurably. Joe's passion for truth, skepticism about proof, and conviction that organizations can solve their risk problems faster by opening themselves to internal conjecture and debate are infectious.

Particular thanks go to the Corporate Executive Board's Scott Bohannon, who not only provided generous encouragement but found creative and efficient ways to keep me involved with board members during the time I spent on the book. I am also grateful to Roger Leeds and Gordon Bodnar at the Johns Hopkins School of Advanced International Studies for allowing me to test some of the ideas in the book through a course on risk management for MA candidates concentrating in finance.

Howard Yoon has been as much a collaborator as a literary agent and inspired much of the practical orientation—with no loss of rigor—that I think is a strength of the book. And Kirsten Sandberg, at Harvard Business School Press, combines sharp substantive judgment and crisp writing to be a gift of an editor. With an incisive creative team like Kirsten and Howard, the book's flaws have to fall all the more glaringly to the author's account.

Instead of the typical remorse-toward-suffering-spouse paragraph, I am happy to report that Ann Marie Moeller gives as well as she gets, and her remarkable book on the language of kimono is due out soon. Her support deserves no fewer thanks for that!

Let me also thank my dear friend Greg Rest for his timely suggestion of the story of Wilmer McLean that opens the book and the Controller Leadership Roundtable's Cigdem Oktem for suggestions on how to tell it; Neil Gaskell for a wonderful interview on his time with Shell in Borneo and, more generally, for years of great advice on financial management; Brian Tsui at the Treasury Leadership Roundtable for his help with the data backing up the chapter 2 sidebar on yield curves; and Stanford's Bob Hall for conversation and advice on his evolving view of how equilibrium sticky wages affect the job-finding rate in recessions.

1

Changing Your Approach to Risk

Two years after marrying Virginia Howe Mason, a rich widow, Wilmer McLean retired from his whole-sale grocery business in the bustling town of Alexandria to a farm called Yorkshire in northern Virginia's Prince William County. Over the next seven years, he and his wealthy bride had two children and entertained friends in grand style. Then in May 1861, Confederate regiments set up camp on the southern part of his farm because of the natural barrier afforded by the stream—called Bull Run—running through it.

Scarcely had General P. G. T. Beauregard asked to use McLean's stone barn on July 18, 1861 when a Federal shell dropped through the farmhouse chimney into a kettle of stew, exploded, and ruined the general's staff lunch.[1] The ensuing skirmish gave little hint of the ferocity of the first battle of Bull Run that would launch real hostilities three days later on McLean's farm.[2]

His proximity to the newly formed Confederate line created an opportunity—building a bigger wholesale business to supply the troops with sugar while living in genteel rural splendor. But high risk attended that opportunity—there was, after all, an army in his back-yard. Still, there might be a way to seize the opportunity and cut the risk. If he relocated closer to the heart of the South's supply chain in Richmond but stayed far enough outside the city, then he might avoid the army altogether and maintain his comfortable landed lifestyle.

So McLean moved his family deep into Virginia. It looked like a smart move at first: the armies would fight both the Second Battle of Bull Run a year later and even a skirmish during Lee's retreat from Gettysburg at Yorkshire.

The next three years were quiet enough for McLean and his wife to produce a third child. But on April 9, 1865, he awoke to columns of butternut-uniformed soldiers marching through the inconsequential village he supposedly chose as a refuge—Appomattox Court House. As McLean watched a nimbus cloud of dust rise from the soldiers' boots in the crossroads, Confederate Colonel Marshall approached him—at random—to ask for the use of a house. When Marshall declined the unfurnished one McLean first proposed, McLean reluctantly offered his own parlor.

There, Confederate General Robert E. Lee and Union General Ulysses Grant negotiated and wrote out the surrender a few hours later. And then began the last contest of the war for McLean—the battle over his parlor furnishings, which quick-thinking officers realized would become invaluable souvenirs.

General Sheridan offered McLean $2.50 for the chair and oval table Grant had used. McLean explained they were not for sale but conceded, "If you choose to take it, you have the physical power to do so."[3] Sheridan took them.

Cavalry officers tried to buy other chairs and seized them when McLean refused. Others cut up upholstery and cane chair backing. Lt. Colonel Thomas W. C. Moore even rode off with a rag doll McLean's daughter Lula had left on the parlor floor. Finally, Union General John Gibbon set up a temporary headquarters in the house for the new Army of the James.

The next day, Brigadier General E. P. Alexander, a distant relative, hailed McLean in surprise and asked what he was doing there in Appomattox. McLean unloaded: "What the hell are *you* doing here? These armies tore my place on Bull Run all to pieces . . . so I just sold out and came here, two hundred miles away, hoping I should never see a soldier again. Now, just look around you! Not a fence-rail is left on the place, the last guns trampled down all my crops, and Lee surrenders in my house."[4] Alexander apologized and blamed the gentlemen on the other side.

Of course, there were no insurance policies that might have covered McLean against the risks of souvenir-seeking soldiers any more than against battle damage. Worse, the end of the war closed his sugar trade. Thus exposed, McLean defaulted on his Appomattox house, and the family returned to Yorkshire. A Richmond bank eventually sold what came to be known as the Surrender House at auction in 1869.

In hindsight, it's not surprising that the war ended up where a sugar broker had moved to trade. After all, Lee's need to resupply determined his movements toward the end of the war, and that meant searching for open rail depots around Richmond. So while McLean's risk of reencountering the Army of Northern Virginia was low, his work as a supplier hardly precluded it. It was a risk others might have been better positioned to weigh.

Weighing risks is the subject of this book. And raising your intelligence about the risks you take—your risk intelligence—is its goal.

Risk intelligence refers to an individual's or an organization's ability to weigh risks effectively. It involves classifying, characterizing, and calculating threats; perceiving relationships; learning quickly; storing, retrieving, and acting upon relevant information; communicating effectively; and adjusting to new circumstances. We can almost always learn something about nonfinancial risks, unlike financial risks that move randomly. The problem is whether we can learn as much as others facing similar risks.

This book is for every manager, entrepreneur, professional, investor, household head, official, administrator, and officer who basically faces McLean's choice. Is an opportunity worth the risk? And it's for everyone who shares McLean's predicament. Can I or my organization learn enough about the risk to benefit from the opportunity?

This might be the larger moral of the story of the man who saw the Civil War start in his backyard and end in his parlor. What seems like a crazy coincidence and therefore unpredictable and uncontrollable may indeed be logical, explicable, and manageable. The trick is finding the best thread of explanation.

It's not as if we don't try. We comb through stacks of information to find needles of insight into risk. But the harder we tug at the threads of explanation, the more our risks seem to unravel in disappointing results. The truth is that we may not be the ones in the best position to understand the risks we take.

FEAR, BOLDNESS, AND RISK SELECTION
IN A DANGEROUS WORLD

Our lives are fraught with risks that seem to expand rather than diminish with scrutiny. Economic and political news stories increasingly give the impression of a world grown newly dangerous, requiring great caution. Our anxiety, not surprisingly, grows steadily.

Over our business and economic risks looms insecurity, partly because neither U.S. action against rogue states nor sympathetic European multiculturalism deals with fanatic individuals. We seem to grow less rather than more able to protect ourselves from the weather even as the best medicines seem to evolve stronger viruses.

We worry about jobs during statistical economic recoveries. Those two miracle economies of the past half century—Germany's and Japan's—rely stubbornly on other people's growth. In the United States, we borrow against the inflated value of our houses as if we were hedge funds but still can't afford our kids' college tuitions. To make ends meet, we double up on jobs, using day care that seemingly makes our children more reckless than sociable. Adding to this anxiety, our leaders—from presidents to prime ministers to Nobel Prize economists—repeatedly warn us to act normally but *very cautiously.*

In the competitive and unforgiving realm of business, however, companies cannot afford a fearful attitude. Most organizations must be bold, not just careful, to survive in a global market. Yet in recent years we have seen brilliant business leaders lose billions—even bring down entire companies—by trying to be *too* aggressive.

We have seen whole categories of Internet companies disappear, the airline and telecommunications industries bottom out, U.S. automaker credit quality fall to the level of junk, and major emerging markets like Brazil, India, South Korea, and China swap places as investment targets overnight. In each case, business and financial leaders have turned bold chances into big losses. But it certainly wasn't from *ignoring* risk.

So neither caution nor boldness alone is satisfactory. Whatever stance we take, unexpected reversals make it seem as though we were playing with loaded dice.

Worse still, the more we learn about the games of chance playing out in the world around us, the higher the house's take seems to rise. It's hard to see how the house edge can rise when the "house" is the whole world. Yet we have little to show for all of the technology and boards of directors' time that companies are throwing at risk management.

For example, a study from the University of Queensland looked at the impact of both risk management practices and boards of directors' attention to them in Australia's one hundred largest public companies between 2000 and 2002. It did find limited evidence that the *quality* of a board's risk oversight affected earnings. But there was no significant impact from the board's involvement in the risk management practices of a company or even its regular review of those practices.[5]

In sum, our risks seem to multiply. Our businesses face technology and geopolitical disruption, and our households face a raft of security risks perhaps more familiar to Wilmer McLean or to Europeans and Asians who lived through World War II or to those living now in the Middle East or in the Balkan States. They multiply whether we adopt a stance of caution or boldness toward them. Our growing ability to measure them and manage them and report them to boards of directors only seems to compound them.

So how can our businesses succeed despite the risks that abound in smarter, faster, and more competitive markets? How can we determine when to be cautious and when to be bold? How can we get smarter about evaluating our personal risks?

We could look at the gap between how much risk we expect and find in any risky initiative or venture. But this is much harder than it looks. You can tell whether your *results* were better than expected. But how do you tell whether the *risk* was greater than expected? This book proposes a simpler gap in our risk assessments: the gap between how well we can learn about an activity's risk and how well others can.

This second gap is a powerful concept. After all, we could be *choosing* risky activities that others are better at learning, regardless of our caution or boldness. We might be *systematically* choosing risks in which we are at some kind of disadvantage. Better risk measurement technology would amplify the benefit of being a fast learner as well as the cost of being a slow one. So gaps between risk learning skills could explain why so few people seem to be beating the odds in the risks they're taking.

Toyota's adoption of just-in-time manufacturing techniques used earlier by Ford provides a concrete example of a firm decisively betting it could close a learning gap—and specifically a gap in learning about production risks. Toyota may even have realized it had a natural advantage that went beyond its access to a superb workforce.

CLOSING THE LEARNING GAP AT TOYOTA
AND TOKYO'S CENTRAL FISH MARKET

Maybe we should call it the Tsukiji production system. In the 1980s I had a chance to tour one of Toyota's five assembly plants near Nagoya, Japan. Each workstation transferred kanban cards to upstream parts-machining stations whenever it completed an assembly. Those cards would trigger more upstream parts production. As you might guess, there were no piles of idle inventory to be seen on the factory floor.

When a parts-machining station at the top of the production line delivered a part in response to a card from an assembly unit, it passed the kanban to the loading dock and triggered an order for more materials. Small vehicles would roar off from the dock to pick up batches of parts and material from suppliers and other Toyota factories nearby.

The tour guide was a little hazy about what happened at the bottom of the production line, where finished cars were rolling out to a huge parking lot. My impression was that someone was actually aggregating sales information from around Japan and launching appropriate kanban cards on their journey up the production line. Since Toyota sold different combinations of cars each hour, the cards led some of the workstations to reconfigure for different vehicles.

The most memorable moment was when the plant manager, after a brief word to the tour guide, removed a number of cards at random from workstations along the production line. The result was a little unpredictable. Until then, most of us had ignored what looked like small traffic lights over each workstation because they were all the same color—green. Now some turned amber or red—but not necessarily right where the manager had removed a card. I think there's always a tiny bit of slack—maybe one extra part set—ready for any station to start working on it. Removing just a few cards exposed where there was no slack at all. As we watched, the manager rebalanced the line, sending workers upstream and down-stream in the direction of the red and amber lights.

After the tour, our group sat around a conference table in stunned silence. It was no surprise that I was stunned, with only an applied economics degree and a few years of strategy consulting under my belt. But there were also some members of Congress in our group, and they had seen the best of American manufacturing techniques many times. They were just as stunned as I was. Toyota seemed to be taking manufacturing to a new level.

In retrospect, what Toyota had taken to a new level was the ability to learn continuously about evolving and emerging risks in its pro-duction system. A generation of American managers would marvel at how *lean* Toyota's inventory was and how *low* its capital costs for financing that inventory were. But that misses the point. Low inven-tory is a means to a greater end at Toyota. It helps expose risks—like the risk that a worker is exhausted, a machine tool wearing down, or a new car configuration too complex—before their effects are really felt. Closing learning gaps about operating risk is what the Toyota production system is really all about.

But that very feat creates a gap for other car companies—namely, the gap in how fast they can learn what engineering problems chang-ing customer needs will create. If car buyers like a combination that's hard to make, Toyota production lines adapt from the bottom up to stay in time with other types of vehicles under assembly. In other systems, it's much harder to resist the temptation just to raise the price of the difficult model.

American carmakers may have misread a lesson here. The lesson seemed to be to follow the customer. After all, real-time customer preferences drive just-in-time systems. But the constant adaptation on a Toyota production line keeps it supple to deal with *unexpected* changes in taste. If you pay attention only to *actual* changes, how can you be sure you're ready for unexpected ones? The new gap in learning speed is proving subtle. It's not just about speed of response to the kinds of changes in customer taste we've seen and maybe even encouraged, but about being ready for *anything*.

For example, Toyota's U.S. strategy diverged sharply from that of its American rivals around 1995. American car buyers seemed to want big vehicles, and American carmakers followed. Everyone knew that tastes could change—that demand for big vehicles might just reflect low gasoline prices, new tax breaks, and persistent price discounts. But it was Toyota that kept tinkering with hybrid technology for small, light, efficient cars—just in case. Just-in-time manufacturing turned into just-in-case manufacturing.

When oil prices started spiking in 2005, everyone recognized a shift in buyer preferences right away. The difference was that Toyota had spent ten years unearthing hybrid vehicle engineering problems and making sure its production lines could handle new ones. Many say General Motors will need years to catch up. It certainly has a gap in its ability to learn about engineering risks in the new technology.

Several days after our Toyota plant visit, I realized I had seen something like it before, but in a hard-to-recognize form. Earlier in the trip, I had woken up at 5 a.m. to visit Tokyo's central fish bazaar, the revered Tsukiji Market. It's big, colorful, and active, and the breakfast sushi's great. You read that it's the biggest fresh fish market in the world. You see countless rows of stalls in all directions devoted to every kind of fish in the world and more things with tentacles than you ever imagined.

And then it hits you. You're surrounded by the most intensive fish distribution system you've ever seen, but you smell no fish. It's not just that the place is clean. It's that nothing is there for *long*. There's no inventory in the stalls, just a few display trays with at least one specimen of each of the stall's specialties. Everything arrives just-in-time, and not because Henry Ford or Ed Deming wrote about it. It's been just-in-time since Tokyo was called Edo in the nineteenth century.

If you buy a few filets, someone whisks the empty tray into a mini-alley behind the stall. Tiny motorized carts zip up and down the alleys and grab what I'll call the kanban trays. Then it's off to the docks nearby, and these are real docks.

Maybe Tsukiji is just optimized to deliver the freshest possible fish to the world's pickiest fish connoisseurs, the restaurant owners who haunt the market. But Tokyo is also famous for the seafood fads that wash over its dining districts from week to week. You'd think that market was too volatile—too risky—for the tiny specialist stalls that fill up Tsukiji. But a system that lets you order your inventory as customers buy it gives you the maximum possible flexibility. Tsukiji learns every day all over again as the morning progresses how the world's biggest and richest city wants to dine.

Taiichi Ohno may be the father of the kanban system.[6] Ford may have used just-in-time techniques on the Model T. But around the time Ohno was graduating from Nagoya Technical High School in the 1930s, Tsukiji Market was rebuilding the sheds that covered its ancient stalls. Toyota's system goes beyond Tsukiji Market's stream-lined customer response times to speed up learning about the *possible* production risks in meeting *possible* customer needs. But it sure owes a debt to Tsukiji Market.

And this raises a key point of this book: *we must know what we're good at learning.* When Kiichiro Toyoda convinced his father in 1936 to move the family manufacturing business out of looms and into automobiles, he would have had some inkling that the tradition of approaching risk by learning fast—imbedded in the core distribution system of Japan's biggest city—was relevant.[7] We can learn from it, too.

This book proposes a practical way to think about risk learning gaps and take action to close or avoid them. Closing those gaps is becoming crucial for anyone whose job involves significant performance responsibility or risky goals. The book is written for management generalists. But risk managers should find even chapter 2's review of risk basics of interest because it challenges conventional wisdom in what for risk is a novel framework: the real-world business competition in which most of us operate every day.

Risks can't really be rising across the board. But through poor risk *selection,* we may be giving an edge to someone else with every risk we take. This is a strong claim, so I'll define the scope of the risks the book covers.

AN ARK OF RISKS

Risk is the possibility of a loss or reversal—or gain or advance— different from what we expect from a decision or an activity. The risks that matter here are the ones that pose a problem in our work or personal lives. We won't spend much time, for example, on the risk of finding more than one kind of restaurant in a lively downtown.

But this book does address the widest possible range of problematic risks. For example, it applies to all of the kinds of business risks listed in figure 1-1.

The list is pretty comprehensive. It includes risks around the acceptance or evaluation of what we provide, here called demand-side risks, and risks around how we produce what we provide, or supply-side risks.

But the scope of the book extends beyond business. Its lessons for running our offices often apply to running our families or even security missions. They apply to any risk that can create a learning gap. It's time to clarify that idea.

LEARNING GAPS AND A DEFINITION OF RISK INTELLIGENCE

One of the central questions about risks is whether and how much we can reduce them by learning more about them. Learning about a risk involves two things. First, it involves the formulation of possible solutions to problems posed by the risk or possible answers to questions about what drives it. Second, it requires experience that can show which solutions may be right, which ones are wrong, or whether we need more options.

Risk intelligence is that *experience*—any and all experience, past and future, that can help us solve problems requiring an understanding of the risk. So as I'm using the term, it's really the second of the two ingredients of learning about risks.

The first, the formulation of possible solutions, is also critically important. Can we explain the risks that pose a threat to our plans? Where do those explanations come from? Are they guesses? If so, how could we evaluate the quality of the guesses we make about the risks we face?[8] Nevertheless, the focus of this book is on what kinds of experience are likely to be most useful in selecting good explanations.

FIGURE 1-1

Types of business risks

Production, or supply-side, risks

- Operating risks like:
  - Control and compliance failures
  - Partner coordination failures
- Supply chain risks like:
  - Supplier failure or political rupture
  - Key cost volatility
- Technology risks like:
  - Infrastructure breakdown
  - Information security breaches
- Workforce risks like:
  - Capacity loss or disruption
  - Key staff loss or defection
- Asset risks like:
  - Fraud or theft
  - Counterparty credit losses

Marketing, or demand-side, risks

- Security or political risks like:
  - Market-disrupting events
  - Geopolitical volatility
- End-market or customer risks like:
  - Brand or reputation erosion
  - Customer consolidation
- Competitive risks like:
  - Disruptive technologies
  - New entrants to the market
- Regulatory or legal risks like:
  - Legislation and litigation
  - Official corruption
- Financial or economic risks like:
  - Financial market volatility
  - Recession

The reason for the focus is that only our imagination really limits the conjectures, models, assumptions, or just plain guesses we advance to explain a risk. Of course, how we organize our businesses to *free* people to envision possible solutions to these shared problems is vital. But the immediate problem of this book is to understand the limits that our current and likely future experience place on what we can learn about a risk. These are limits that mental audacity cannot always overcome. They are fixed by whom we must meet and how we must spend our time to do our jobs.

So if we must allocate scarce time to problems or tasks, we'll be better off knowing what kind of risk problems our current or likely future experience can help us solve. Risk intelligence is about making choices bearing the risks that our natural run of experience can really penetrate.

Of course, this is easier said than done. Well-worn myths about risk constantly tempt us to take up project or activity risks we're not very good at learning. But there are four rules of risk intelligence that can keep those myths in check.

FOUR RULES OF RISK INTELLIGENCE
AND THE MYTHS THEY EXPLODE

The rules of risk intelligence resist myths that can and do keep us from succeeding in the face of risk. Each of these myths is appealing; overcoming their temptation is hard. As a memory aid, the first letters of the rules spell out *risk*.

Separate chapters of this book show how to carry out each of the rules: chapter 2 offers a guideline for the first rule, and chapters 3, 4, and 5 lay out practical tools for following the others. They prove there really are practical ways to think about what we can learn and how it should affect our risk taking. The rest of this introductory chapter outlines the myths, the rules of risk intelligence that explode them, and the chapters that implement the rules.

MYTH 1: ALL RISKS ARE RANDOM

This may sound reasonable, but it's wrong. The source of uncertainty in most risks is that we don't know what determines them. For example, coin flips *appear* random. But there's little doubt that with enough information about the toss of a specific coin, we could predict how it will land. The uncertainty arises because we normally don't know all there is to know about the toss.

Random risks, however, are indeterminate: *no* knowledge will reduce their uncertainty. For example, most analysts think the movements of securities markets are truly random. So in a sense, there is less to know about random risks.

But if there's less to know about random risks, why are nonrandom ones so hard to manage? The problem may be that we don't understand them as well as random risks.

One reason we don't understand them is that we usually learn our lessons on risk from banks. Banks have a long history of managing financial risks predating Ken Arrow's seminal work on complete markets in the middle of the twentieth century. But financial risks are mostly random. Since nonrandom risks pose challenges far different from random ones, the financial risk management perspective can be dangerously misleading. For example, it ignores competitive differences in judging risks.

And this gets at the other reason we don't understand nonrandom risks very well. With nonrandom risks, every risk taker is in a different position to learn about what drives them. So for every nonrandom risk, some risk takers can reduce their uncertainty more than others. If the situation is competitive, this will affect the economics of the risk. It may even create a "leader takes all" opportunity.

Chapter 2 defines these nonrandom, learnable risks and develops the first rule of risk intelligence:

Rule 1. Recognize which risks are learnable.

MYTH 2: SINCE RISKS AVERAGE OUT, THEY RARELY CREATE PERSISTENT WINNERS AND LOSERS

We could all just muddle along if only this were true. One of the main claims of this book, however, is that nonrandom, or learnable, risks *do* create winners and losers. We can never hope to build an experience or information base that will let us stay on top of every risk. But there will probably always be some risks we are geared to master.

It's hard to let go of this myth. It means risk is no excuse. No one can *guarantee* risky results. But wise choices could lead us to risks we are good at evaluating, and unwise choices could lead us to risks we are bad at evaluating. So we must choose well.

But if we can excel at evaluating some risks, why can't we excel at evaluating all or most of them? Surely some experiences and information have *intrinsic* value—they apply to almost any risk problem. After all, we all have experiences that we consider fundamental. We all have had experiences that were deeply surprising, that rocked us, and that we imagine applying repeatedly to different situations in our lives. Similarly, information theorists treat improbable results as the most valuable ones.

But this ignores relevance. We must ask how relevant our current and likely future experiences are to the risk problem we're trying to solve. That will depend not only on the experiences but also on the problem and the solutions we think might solve it.

Even a strong impression can be irrelevant. Suppose you design your commute to avoid repeating a terrible experience with a backup on a downtown bridge. You reckon that no matter how much traffic patterns change, the possibility such a backup will recur keeps your experience relevant. But say you shift your work hours. Now different roads are open, and you wonder whether the bridge might be less subject to backups than your new alternatives. You may find that your backup experience isn't really relevant to your new options. Indeed, new options change the relevance of old information.

Any measure of how well our experiences position us to learn about a kind of risk must balance these two factors. It must consider the relevance of our experiences to the risk as well as how improbable or surprising they are. Chapter 3 proposes a risk intelligence score for each major risk we face. It lets us select the projects whose risks we can likely assess best and manage successfully.

What happens to the winner and loser myth if everyone starts using risk intelligence scores to make business choices? If our success in managing a project's risk depends on the relevance of our experiences to it, every risk potentially gives rise to a new playing field. After all, each new project, activity, or line of business raises the possibility that a new set of experiences will be most relevant to its risks. Some will find their most vital experiences irrelevant to the new risks; others will find new relevance in experiences they usually ignore. So every risk draws a new line between those most and least able to learn about it.

This could therefore be the rare business advice book where the advice would actually work better if *everyone* followed it. If everyone used risk intelligence scores to pursue the risks their experience let them understand best, then productivity would rise across all projects bearing those risks. Fewer people would be disappointed by business portfolios that were losing across the board.

Chapter 3 proposes a measure of our ability to learn about any kind of nonrandom risk in order to implement the second rule of risk intelligence:

Rule 2. Identify risks you can learn about fastest.

MYTH 3: THERE'S NO PATTERN TO HOW RISKS EVOLVE

This book argues that nonrandom risks—just like innovations, hobbies, technologies, romances, projects, lines of business, after-school activities, and products—have natural life cycles. This has a big impact on how we should select risky projects and activities. It raises the question of what hidden challenges risk life cycles actually pose.

Chapter 4 argues that two forces act on any major project or activity risk. One, of course, is the risk taker's evolving risk intelligence regarding the risk. The other is the extent to which the risk diversifies all the other risks that the risk taker faces. Here's how these forces give rise to distinct stages in the natural life cycle of a risk.

To begin, we try to improve our risk intelligence regarding the major risks in some high-priority activity. If things work out, our success in the activity raises the profile of its risks. So as their impact on our overall risk grows, individual risks that may initially increase the diversification of our overall risk eventually dominate it and decrease its diversification.

But this means success *always* exposes us to competition. Not only do bolts from the blue like disruptive technologies threaten successful initiatives. Anytime we succeed in some activity or line of business, our exposure to its risks *must* grow. But that allows newcomers to try out small-scale experiments in the same activity or line of business. If the experiments are small enough, they will not really affect the newcomers' overall risk profile. From an investor's perspective, therefore, the experiments are risk free, and the newcomer can finance them more cheaply than we can.

This brings us to the third stage of a natural risk life cycle. At some point, the newcomers may make enough noise to reduce the attractiveness of our project. If so, we will stop investing in the learning needed to stay abreast of the project's risks. Those risks will have evolved through a natural life cycle of rising risk intelligence, falling diversification, and then falling risk intelligence. The pattern holds even if no one disrupts the activity with some new discovery or technology.

IBM's mainframe computing business is a classic example. In the first stage, IBM developed a preeminent understanding of the risks in mainframe technology and customer usage. Next, IBM's mainframe business grew to the point where you could identify the risks of the company with the risks of mainframes.

At this point, other technology companies started to dabble in industrial computing. As long as their experiments stayed small and they diversified their other businesses, they could afford to play catch-up. Sun would go on to carve out a position in servers. Cisco would dominate network infrastructure.

IBM faced other challenges, especially the rise of personal computing and the migration of profits to software. But in the end, its dominance in mainframe computing could not offset its overexposure to the risks of the mainframe business. Its need to diversify led Lou Gerstner to reposition the company in large-scale computing solutions.

Risk life cycles create a hidden challenge. When you compare the life cycle stages of your major risks, you see they form a *pipeline*. As with any pipeline, bottlenecks and gaps raise problems. For example, you could be pursuing too many projects that require intensive learning at the same time. Or you might have left such a large gap between risks that you have no new projects coming to fruition where you enjoy a risk intelligence advantage when you need them.

Chapter 4 will reveal where your major risks are in their life cycles. The result is a picture of your risk pipeline that highlights where you have taken on too many risks posing new learning challenges and where you may be developing too few new risk skills to stay competitive. The risk strategy audits provide a practical way to implement the third rule of risk intelligence:

Rule 3. Sequence risky projects in a "learning pipeline."

MYTH 4: BUSINESS PARTNERS GET THE SAME RESULTS NO MATTER HOW THEY ALLOCATE RISK

Most products require distribution networks. Think of where you bought (or are reading) this book. The company that produces something may not be the best one to retail it. Similarly, the company that incurs a risk may not be the best one to bear it. So risks need distribution networks for much the same reason that products do.

Of course, we can't evade a risk altogether by leaving it to our customers or suppliers. The price we pay for something rises for every risk we pass to suppliers. The price we realize falls for every risk our products or services impose on our customers. But *all three will benefit* if we can distribute each risk to whoever can best absorb it. So those customers and suppliers create a natural distribution network for each major risk.

This matters not only for learnable risks but for random risks, like sensitivity to stock prices. Unlike learnable risks, random risks give rise to no strong advantages or disadvantages in risk assessment. As a result, the level of cooperation in our risk networks can be an especially important advantage in activities with random risks.

Chapter 5 shows how to identify the ideal role we should play in our risk networks for each of our major risks. It lays out a tool called a risk-role matrix that gives a snapshot of all the roles our risks are pushing us to adopt. By showing which risks' ideal roles converge, such a matrix can help us decide which risks we ought to pursue.

The risk-role matrix also makes tangible the notion of *risk ecologies* among customers, suppliers, and competitors for each of our activities or lines of business. Risk ecologies raise the issue of how relevant the guidance and feedback of our current customers may be to managing the risks of the larger markets we target. For example, someone who creates outrageous print ads for the Manhattan market might have a tough time launching an agency in a quiet midwestern town. The urban feedback that molded her style may not be relevant to advertising in a place like Cincinnati.

This chapter broadens the scope from our own risk intelligence to the risk intelligence of our network. It gives a model for the ideal risk roles that our initiatives call on us and our customers and suppliers to play. The risk-role matrices it introduces develop the fourth rule of risk intelligence:

Rule 4. Keep networks of partners to manage all risks.

RISK INTELLIGENCE AND CORE COMPETENCIES

Like its namesake *emotional intelligence,* risk intelligence is not really an innate talent or an intellectual aptitude.[9] It's more like a variation on market intelligence or even security intelligence. That's not a bad thing. We can always improve the kind of intelligence that depends on ongoing observation, exploration, and learning.

Nor is risk intelligence limited to individuals. It includes all the experiential and information resources we can bring to bear on identifying a solution to a risk problem. Those resources are irreducibly social. You might even say risks provide the *commercial or social context* that makes some of those resources more valuable than others.

Risk intelligence is therefore a little like a core competency of an individual, a team, or an organization. It's narrower than experience or information in general. But it's broader than any specific bit of practical know-how. It consists of whatever collective experience can help determine the evolving drivers of a risk.

There are three reasons to question the applicability of innate talent to risk. First, the importance of relevance to risk intelligence means the value of experience really depends on what problems we're trying to solve. There's nothing universal about it. So every new problem creates opportunities for experiences far from what the best educations can hope to encompass. Risk problems seem open ended.

Moreover, our experience is relevant to the choice among the solutions we have devised to our risk problems. If we propose new solutions, new experiences may become important in evaluating them. For that reason, the value of our experiences may change even if our problems do not. So risk solutions seem open ended, too.

Finally, what's true of risk intelligence may be true of other "core competencies" that organizations identify in managing risk. Those competencies that involve managerial judgment will probably prove just as contextual as risk intelligence. In fact, there may be no such thing as innate talent when it comes to dealing with risk.

That's why intelligence agencies cultivate diverse and sometimes bizarre sources of information. The contrast between *conflicting* U.S. intelligence agency views and *unequivocal* White House assertions on Saddam Hussein's weapon systems prior to the Iraq War is instructive. Intelligence officials frequently warned reporters that Saddam might have to pretend he had weapons to avoid invasion by hostile neighbors. That relevant consideration never appeared in the administration's public deliberations.

The seemingly chaotic practices of intelligence services may hold a useful lesson for firms whose pursuit of global growth opportunities is forcing them to embrace increasingly diverse risks. Even the *idea* that risk intelligence is more like access to a diverse reservoir of experience than a definable aptitude may separate winners and losers.

This should provide grounds for optimism even as our risks seem to multiply under the lens of better information technology. The good news is that we need not identify hidden aptitudes or talents for dealing with risk. But we must keep an open mind about what kind of learning may help us solve our evolving risk problems.

Perhaps we shouldn't be surprised at this conclusion. Risk stories rarely seem to end up as badly as they start out. For example, historians with a romantic streak like telling of Wilmer McLean's ultimate destitution. It's true only up to a point. He did give up the farm at Bull Run. In the end, however, he returned to Alexandria to work for the Internal Revenue Service and the U.S. Bureau of Customs until 1880. Maybe the Federals socialized his risk after all.

2

Separating Learnable Risks from Random Ones in Business Decisions

Have you noticed that no one ever seems to ask whether our risks are random? Shouldn't it matter? After all, the two possible sources of a risk's uncertainty are quite distinct. Something truly random may be going on. Or it may just be too hard to learn more about it.

This chapter draws a distinction between nonrandom risks—which it defines as *learnable*—and random ones. It explains why the distinction matters for understanding when our *relative* risk assessment skills may affect results. In doing so, it reviews the basic risk management framework, but its emphasis on the comparative and competitive dimension of risk assessment should be of interest to specialists in the field as well as generalists trying to make better decisions under uncertainty.

An example shows just how often we overlook this distinction between random and nonrandom risks. A friend who runs accounting for the manufacturing division of a big U.S. equipment maker describes the day his company's new risk officer announced an "enterprise risk initiative." The initiative would end up asking everything about the company's risks except whether we can predict them.

A form accompanied the announcement in an urgent-looking pink envelope. "Describe your risks," it insisted, giving three categories. *Market risk*—that would be interest rate or foreign exchange risk, neither of which greatly affected my friend's division. *Credit risk*—my friend marked this since one of his distributors seemed fragile. *Business risk*—this one looked as if it meant everything else.

Next came a request to estimate typical and worst-case losses from each of the division's most frequent or severe risks. Then there was a request to "estimate the market correlation of the worst risks." But nowhere did it ask how well managers felt they understood the risks or whether they were purely random or just hard to predict.

"Ridiculous," was my friend's verdict. Asking about correlation was like asking whether some of the risks canceled each other out—a break for the manager. But why should the company offer a break without checking how well managers understood their risks? In fact, a manager who was confused about the business environment might actually *worsen* correlation by neglecting her unique risks whenever a market-correlated risk caused a loss.

In the end, he sat on the survey until someone in the marketing division managed to kill it. That took about a week.

The point isn't that the company forgot to ask about the probability of the divisions' risks. In fact, it picked up much of that information by asking about worst-case losses. The point is that it didn't ask which risks might be susceptible to further analysis and which ones were just plain unpredictable no matter what.

Of course, it would have been shocking if the risk office *had* asked which risks were random and which ones were not. The not-so-unusual oversight reflects the recent history of risk management as something of a financial specialty, especially since Markowitz's 1952 paper on how risks diversify one another in a stock portfolio.[1]

For banks and investors, nearly every risk that matters outside credit risk really is random. This is because most of the risks that have historically concerned financial institutions come from price variables in so-called complete markets. These are markets where prices reflect all relevant publicly available information. Stock market indexes, one-year interest rates, and euro–dollar exchange rates are examples. Since complete markets incorporate all available information, it's impossible to predict where they will go next. So risks driven by market prices are truly random.

Risk management is just as important to the rest of a modern economy, however, and it's by no means clear that the risks other businesses need to manage are random like most financial risks. Sales estimates are a notorious example. A lawn-and-garden firm acquiring a line of insect repellants needs to know how much new product it can hope to sell. There's significant risk that any market estimate may be wrong. But if we knew enough about our potential customer base, we could reduce or even eliminate the uncertainty. There's a business risk here, but the uncertainty behind it isn't random.

This chapter makes the case that if we want to manage the risks underlying most parts of a modern business or its growth opportunities, we must separate what I'll call learnable risks from the truly random ones. In fact, it's worth calling this out as the first rule of risk intelligence:

Rule 1. Recognize which risks are learnable.

To see why this separation has become so important, we need to define the terms a little more carefully.

A DEFINITION THAT'S LEARNABLE

For the purposes of this book, *learnable* risks are the ones we could make less uncertain if we had the time and resources to learn more about them. That leaves *random* risks defined as those that no analysis of causes or drivers can make less uncertain. What drives them is truly stochastic.

At first, it might seem that *all* risks are random. After all, they reflect uncertainty. But uncertainty doesn't require truly random processes. Limits to our knowledge also give rise to uncertainty. When they do, the resulting risk is learnable.

Risks based on major exchange rates, for example, appear to be largely random. They are random in the sense that if someone could routinely predict their direction, she could wring unlimited profits out of foreign exchange trades. Yet no one does that. Market prices reflect new information too quickly.

As I write this, in fact, I am losing an office pool on the exchange rate for the euro in U.S. dollars. For me, the risk is a small bet. But for a company that sells consumer packaged goods like olive oil, dried pasta, or nuts, a failure of the dollar to drop to an exchange rate at which U.S. exports become more competitive can be a big risk. The firm's U.S. plants may be unable to turn a profit on, say, almonds sold to Europe. The fact that the underlying foreign exchange risk is random means no one can predict how many jars of almonds the firm will be able to export profitably from the United States to Europe. Any company with a similar exposure will face a risk of the same magnitude.

Contrast this exchange rate risk with risk reflecting exposure to bad weather or natural catastrophes. Are weather and other natural risks as random as the risks reflecting market prices seem to be?

The tsunami that struck the rim of the Indian Ocean at the end of 2004 and claimed over two hundred fifty thousand victims, for example, seemed as tragically unpredictable as any natural disaster. In fact, the Indian Ocean had been relatively calm since Krakatoa erupted in 1883. Yet natural disasters aren't random the way market movements are.

The difference is not that anyone could have predicted the tsunami in detail. What matters is that it was possible to know at least a little about it in advance. In the case of the Indian Ocean tsunami, once researchers based in Hawaii had connected the original shock from an underwater earthquake with a report of shoreline damage in Sumatra, they inferred that a wave was speeding westward across the Indian Ocean that could do damage to Sri Lanka and India. One of the tragedies is that Indian Ocean countries had no protocols for acting on this kind of warning.

Moreover, researchers had recorded seismic activity in the area prior to the earthquake. Again, this doesn't mean we were in a position to predict that a tsunami was imminent. But we knew a little. It shows that the uncertainty underlying natural catastrophes reflects limits on what we know rather than irreducible randomness. That means it's at least possible to reduce the uncertainty around these events if we can figure out a cost-effective way to gather more relevant information about their causes.

This is what's really at stake in separating truly random risks from other risks. The question is whether we could reduce their underlying uncertainty by gathering more information. To put it another way, what matters here is whether it's possible to *learn* anything that could systematically reduce the scope of the uncertainty underlying a risk or even transform it into a predictable certainty.

In sum, I'll call risks learnable if it's possible at least in principle to learn things that make them less uncertain. Random risks would then be the ones where *nothing* we could learn would reduce the uncertainty behind them.

WHAT YOUR BANKER DOESN'T KNOW ABOUT RISK

We can start to put the distinction to work right away. It explains why the lessons banks and investors learned about risk since 1950 won't solve all *our* problems with nonfinancial risks. Here, for instance, are four challenges we face in handling learnable risks every day that don't apply to the random risks banks face.

- First, two people may disagree on the *size* of a learnable risk and may keep disagreeing about it. For example, a contractor who lives in the Mississippi Delta may size up the natural hazards of Hurricane Katrina reconstruction work in the bayous around New Orleans very differently from an outside contractor. The gap may persist even if they work together, especially if the local contractor uses his experience to observe work-site conditions more sharply than the visitor.

  But no bank can estimate the likely impact of interest rate changes on a book of loans and deposits any better than the next. Interest rate changes are truly random, even if their variability doesn't change much from year to year. So all a bank can do is figure the impact of that historical variability on the particular loans and deposits in its books. From time to time, someone like George Soros may have an insight into rate movements. But nobody wins consistently. Even Soros lost $2 billion in 1998.[2]

- Second, two people may differ persistently on *what to do* about a learnable risk. They're especially likely to differ if they keep disagreeing on how big it is. An alligator crossing a dyke a hundred yards away between bayou impoundments may tree our visiting contractor without fazing the local.

  But it's hard to imagine one bank consistently hedging the random risk in its net interest margin (the spread between its loan and deposit rates) differently from another bank with similar loans and deposits. They are equally in the dark about how interest rates are going to change, and have equal access to the historical variability of those rates. So they're likely to reach similar conclusions about controlling the risk.

- Third, two people with differing experience of a learnable risk should probably expect *different returns* from taking it.

This is because differences in how they assess the risk will probably lead them to manage it differently. But if their management approaches to it diverge, then the returns they extract from taking the risk will probably differ. So while our Delta visitor and native both avoided the alligator in the last example, the visitor expended far more effort—and over time might incur more unnecessary costs—for the same result.

Financial institutions, on the other hand, can expect a stable relationship between random risks and the rewards for taking them. Any two banks with similar loan and deposit books, for instance, will probably derive similar results from their positions over time. If the randomness of interest rate risk leads them to similar risk assessments (because you can't improve on them), and if those assessments lead to similar management tactics, then their results will simply have to track.

- Fourth and finally, the returns someone gets from a learnable risk may depend on *who else is taking the risk.* This is because the experience of other risk takers affects the prices they will accept for the risky service or activity. The risk taker who assesses the risk most efficiently can set a price for whatever product the risky activity produces, or set an expectation for risky outcomes that may be hard for others to match. So the price each risk taker can realize from work subject to the risk may depend on how good other risk takers are at making judgments about it.

The bayou reconstruction example provides a homely but exact illustration of this. Imagine a visiting contractor spending money on personal safety precautions that the local contractor considers unnecessary. As long as he's right about the risk, the local contractor can set a price that the visitor considers unprofitable.

Financial institutions can manage portfolios of random risks without regard to other risk takers. This is because no institution can create a persistent pricing advantage from its predictions about the risk. So a good estimate of results will depend only on which risks are in the portfolio and not on who else is taking them. Any two banks with similar portfolios should have similar results.

What's interesting and even a little shocking is that learnable risks seem to violate basic assumptions that banks safely make for random risks. So the first order of business in having more success with risk is separating learnable and truly random risks.

But before turning to this, we must sharpen one more definition. It involves what is truly unique to random risks. Specifically, we must clarify that the randomness of a risk limits what people can learn about its drivers. It doesn't necessarily limit what they can do to manage it. For example, two banks will generally make the same assessment of a random risk, like an interest rate exposure. And to the extent that how they manage that risk depends on their assessment of it, they will manage it the same way. But they may still develop generally different management approaches.

This is not true for learnable risks. People will differ in how they assess them as well as how they manage them.

So the crucial distinction between learnable and random risks is not about how to manage them. There is always something to learn about managing every risk. We can improve response times, train people to recognize signs that something has gone wrong, and even control the size of our exposure. Whether a particular risk is learnable or random thus has little to do with our ability to manage it.

The point of separating learnable and random risks is *cognitive:* it involves finding out what drives them. What we can learn about controlling them is critically important, but it doesn't explain what's different about them. We must separate them because of what we can learn about the causes of learnable ones and how uncertain they are. So let's avoid calling a risk learnable just because we think we can control it or manage it better. That's not what distinguishes learnable risks.

"Bank Risk Taking, Yield Curves, and Monetary Impotence" takes a closer look at the interest rate environment in which savers, banks, and borrowers operate. It shows that nonrandom, learnable risks can and do affect economic outcomes just as powerfully as purely random risks such as interest rate variability. It also offers a framework for thinking about the role bank lending plays in shaping interest rates when savers are risk averse—a role that is surprising given bank loans' relatively small share of modern credit markets.

The next main order of business is: why superior risk assessment is so important for learnable risks. Readers who want to dig right into it can skip the sidebar without losing the thread of the argument.

LEARN BEFORE YOU LEAP

We must assess risks to know how hard to try to control them. This means scoping out the losses they could cause. For learnable risks, differences in how well people do this are growing as some take better advantage of what they know.

The skeptical reader might say, "Look, David, I can see why you would want to focus on risks we might *manage* better. But you're separating learnable and random risks to find the ones we might *assess* better. Why categorize risks if we're not doing it to prioritize our risk *management* efforts?"

The answer is that before we start to work on managing our risks better, we must determine which risks we're going to tackle. For example, every time a drug firm looks at a new drug development project or initiative, management must decide which risks they want

Bank Risk Taking, Yield Curves, and Monetary Impotence

Here's a framework for thinking about interest rates that shows learnable risks are just as "real" as random ones. It's similar to economists' "preferred habitat" models in assuming that people's expectations and present needs both affect rates.

The *yield curve,* meaning the difference between long-term and short-term interest rates, can reflect how much risk both savers and banks are taking. Partly, this difference (also called the steepness of the yield curve) reflects inflation expectations. If people think inflation will rise, they expect higher long-term interest rates to compensate. Since inflation is often a sign of rising consumption and investment, market watchers and economists traditionally link steep yield curves with an accelerating economy.

The data in the graph in figure 2-1, however, presents a puzzle. With the steepness of the yield curve (not the absolute level of rates) on the vertical axis and the growth of commercial and industrial (C&I) bank lending on the horizontal axis, it frankly looks like a mess. Each dot reflects a month's annualized C&I loan growth and the yield curve as a bank might see it at the beginning of the month—the difference between the rate on a long-term loan to a BBB-rated company and the three-month risk-free rate on U.S. Treasury securities (standing in for the rate banks pay to depositors). But while you would expect it to be a mess, you might also expect it to "lean" to the right. You might expect periods of faster C&I loan growth to coincide with steeper yield curves reflecting inflation expectations in an accelerating economy.

The trouble is that it leans the wrong way. Higher business loan growth is linked to flatter yield curves. There's no evidence for a causal connection, but you wonder. No obvious model would imply that flat yield curves cause economic or at least loan growth. If anything, you might expect flat yield curves to discourage bank

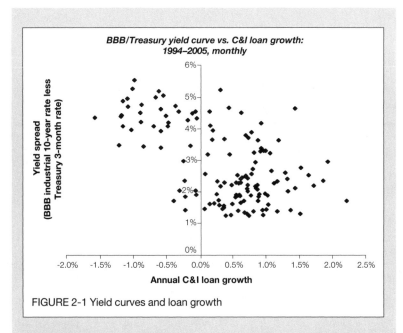

FIGURE 2-1 Yield curves and loan growth

lending because they reduce the net interest income banks can earn as a reward for taking the risk that interest rates on their deposits might rise suddenly. There is, however, a model implying that faster loan growth might cause the yield curve to flatten.

In general, savers prefer investing short-term for liquidity, while businesses prefer issuing longer-term loans or bonds for stability. But when the yield curve gets steeper—higher on the graph in figure 2-2—savers will substitute long-term savings for short-term savings. So the short-term-savings curve is downward sloping. Issuers will substitute short-term loans or bonds. So the short-term-issuance curve slopes up.

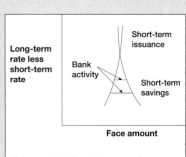

FIGURE 2-2 Short-term saving, short-term issuance, and bank intermediation

(continued)

Banks help bridge the gap between the short-term savings that savers prefer and the long-term issuance that businesses prefer. The length of the horizontal bridging lines reflects how much short-term-deposit money banks are investing in longer-term loans. The longer the line, the more risk banks take of short-term rates going one way and long-term rates going the other. The height of the line reflects the steepness of the yield curve. So the higher the line, the more net interest income banks should earn on at least their fixed-rate loans. From the banking system's point of view, in other words, the length of the line corresponds to risk, and the height corresponds to rewards.

This means that more bank risk taking—a longer line on the graph—corresponds to flatter yield curves. It makes sense, since bank willingness to take risk lets savers keep more short-term deposits, while businesses take more long-term loans.

Central bank activity affects the short-term-savings curve. When a central bank tightens monetary policy, the curve shifts left and squeezes the bank activity line down. This corresponds to higher short-term interest rates and a flatter yield curve.

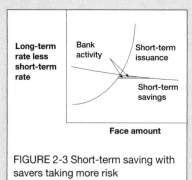

FIGURE 2-3 Short-term saving with savers taking more risk

But what happens when savers become more willing to tie up their money in longer-term investments if rates are attractive? What happens when they become willing to "take back" some of that risk from banks? Then the graph looks like the one in figure 2-3.

In this situation, the central bank cannot have much of an impact on short-term savings. (A flat savings curve looks much the same when you shift it to the right or left.) If the central bank prints money and depresses short-term rates, risk-taking savers shift money quickly into longer-term deposits or stocks. So the difference between long-term and short-term rates doesn't get much wider and the yield curve remains stable. Standard macroeconomic theory suggests other consequences would include less sensitivity of the economy to oil price shocks and more sensitivity to budget and current account deficits.

Conversely, volatile yield curves indicate that savers are shouldering less risk (a steeper savings curve). This initially implies greater central bank effectiveness.

Such effectiveness shows up when yield curves flatten after a central bank tightens money (from 1 to 2 in figure 2-4). Flat yield curves then normally discourage longer-term bank lending until long-term rates rise and the yield curve steepens again. The graph pictures this as a simultaneous shortening and rise in the bank activity line (3 in figure 2-4).

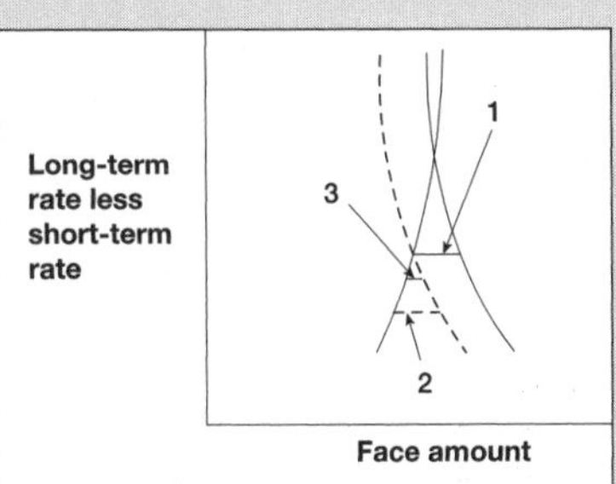

Even when a central bank

FIGURE 2-4 Effects of central bank activity

tightens money effectively and flattens the yield curve, though, it's possible that banks won't respond. This would happen if banks ignored the reduced margins they were earning on short-term deposits invested in longer-term loans. For example, banks trying to grow fee-based businesses would become less sensitive to the risk-reward trade-off in fixed-rate business loans if the loans helped secure fees.

This suggests an explanation for the failure of long-term dollar rates to rise as the Federal Reserve raised short-term rates 3½ percent

(continued)

through 2004 and 2005. The Fed's chairman, Alan Greenspan, called it a conundrum in February 2005; then-governor Ben Bernanke blamed a global savings glut (even though such gluts normally accompany global slowdowns); and St. Louis Fed president William Poole read it as stable expectations.[3] Whatever the cause, though, intermediaries were extending long-term credit. This is just what you might expect if U.S. banks relied on the new kinds of fee business allowed under the Gramm-Leach-Bliley Act to cover the risk of interest rate losses on their loans.

In such a case, long-term rates would fail to rise, and the yield curve would fail to resume its steepness after the central bank tightened money. The graph would picture this as a bank activity line that failed to shorten and rise even after being squeezed down (staying at 2 in the graph in figure 2-4). It would indicate that banks were absorbing more risk even though savers were not. And once again, it implies reduced central bank effectiveness.

The twin cases of savers and banks absorbing more risk suggest nonrandom risks are just as real as random ones. Banks, of course, take interest rate risk. Savers, however, take the risk of running low in cash and in their bank accounts when they might need them. This risk of illiquidity does not have the purely random character of the interest rate risk banks take. But it has an equally real effect on the economy.

to bear. It makes sense to ask whether those risks reflect random factors or limits on what the firm knows about future needs and business conditions.

But there's more to my skeptical reader's question: "Why does it matter what *drives* the risk? Surely all that matters is whether it's manageable."

Suppose the drug company in the example knows equally well how to manage the risks in launching a stress drug and a malaria drug. The question is whether the nature of those risks makes a difference even if the company can manage them equally well. Let's expand the example to see why you might want to choose one risk and avoid another even though you can manage them to exactly the same level of worst-case loss.

Say the market size for the stress drug is random—maybe it's for traders, and we think demand will depend on whether the stock market goes up or down. The market for the malaria drug is uncertain, too, but perhaps because it treats a new kind of malaria. Then the launch of the stress drug is subject principally to a random risk, while the launch of the malaria drug is subject to a learnable one. Why does it matter, so long as you manage them equally well?

It matters because you could lose money if you're wrong about the malaria drug's level of risk and someone else is right. Of course, nobody can be "right" about the stress drug, except sporadically and by accident, since everyone's equally in the dark about the future of the stock market. But the differing assessments possible for the malaria drug's learnable risks could lead to very different results for equally capable risk managers.

To see how differing assessments can lead to differing results, imagine the drug company in the example raises money against the launch risk of its malaria drug. It may want to provide for extra testing and advertising in case uptake is low. The drug's *perceived* launch risk then determines how much money the firm must set aside.

Its competitors do the same thing. But if the risks in this therapeutic area are learnable, then some of those competitors may finance their launch more efficiently. What's different about the stress drug is that competitors will have no basis for forecasting the level of launch risk more accurately—and thus pricing it more efficiently—since no one has a privileged view into where the stock market is going.

We must scope the risks that our choices present all the time, whether our company is undertaking an acquisition, or our division is undertaking a new project, or our office is improving a business process, or the family is thinking about a new kitchen. In fact, it's hard to imagine any kind of risk that doesn't raise questions about the scope of the uncertainty in whatever project or activity gives rise to it.

When it comes to random risks, there's no basis for inconsistent answers. But we may be singularly bad at gauging the impact of a particular learnable risk, while others are quite good at it. Failing to understand which of our risks are learnable and avoiding the learnable ones we can't learn well could have a huge impact on our results.

BOEING, AIRBUS, AND THE ECONOMICS OF ASSESSING LEARNABLE RISKS

In early 2001, Boeing canceled development of a stretch jumbo jet it had announced three years earlier. The episode is a dramatic case of a company basing a strategic decision on not just its assessment of the risks but also its *ability* to assess them. Some say it was the beginning of the end for then-CEO Phil Condit, too. It certainly pitted opposite personalities against one another in Condit and new Airbus CEO Noël Forgeard.

The ability to assess or scope out risks may sound more like an investment concern than a factor in making risky decisions. There certainly are similarities. We must select our investments carefully to make sure uncertain benefits are worth the present cost. Similarly, we must select our risks carefully to make sure the expected benefit is worth uncertain costs. In fact, the growing study of information economics deals with risk assessment largely by comparing how much information reduces the scope or size of a risk to a reduction in the up-front cost of an investment, and then calculating the impact of the reduction on the returns the risk taker can expect.

There's a limit to the parallel, however. The impact of Boeing's ability to assess a learnable risk on its decision to take that risk is quite different from the reasons to take random risks like investing in the stock market. It's more like whether your eye for real estate justifies spending time improving and flipping houses.

Suppose, for example, you make a list of potential real estate projects and other business alternatives. You sift through it and find a range of risks. If you understand the scope of the risks in the real estate projects, you can choose the ones with the highest likely returns adjusted for the possibility something will go wrong. You can also look to see whether your competitors' knowledge of the local real estate market limits the returns you can hope to extract. So scoping risks helps you select attractive properties, while understanding how well you scope those risks helps you decide whether to play the real estate game in the first place. The story of Airbus and Boeing suggests *understanding* how well you assess a risk may be as important as how well you assess it.

The cancellation was surprising because Boeing had reconfirmed its plans for a stretch jumbo two years earlier in 1999. But three other factors made it remarkable. First, the stakes of letting Airbus dominate the market for very large aircraft with its proposed A380 superjumbo were huge. Second, if Boeing couldn't win with its huge cost advantage in jumbos, where *could* it win? And third, Condit and Forgeard were polar opposites and seemed destined to compete head-on.

There was little question about the stakes. Airbus and Boeing both seemed to agree that there was room for only one competitor in the market for very large aircraft—aircraft even larger than 747s with four hundred to five hundred seats. Airbus dominance of the segment would "dislodge Boeing as the market leader in commercial aircraft after more than 40 years of market dominance."[4]

And Boeing's cost advantage appeared to be substantial. Airbus laid out $11.9 billion to launch the A380 superjumbo.[5] Boeing estimated it could launch a stretch version of the 747 for just $4 billion.[6]

The cost advantage was no surprise: Boeing already had a similar product.

Finally, Condit was the quintessential all-American business leader. He chaired the Business Roundtable, headed an Aeronautics Advisory Committee for NASA, and presided over the Chief Seattle Council of the Boy Scouts of America. He had engineering degrees from Berkeley and Princeton. He was lead engineer of a new 747 configuration in 1968 and chief project engineer for the 757 ten years later. He even had a patent for flexible aircraft sailwings.[7] And he could get along with almost anyone.

By all reports, he even got along with Officier de la Légion d'Honneur, Officier de l'Ordre National du Mérite, and Knight Commander of the Order of the British Empire Noël Forgeard. Forgeard graduated from the elite Ecole Polytechnique to serve in the French Ministries of Industry, Transportation, and Defense. Later he became an adviser for industrial affairs to then-prime minister Jacques Chirac.[8] Central to his career was the French vision of an industrial policy-making government as an active partner of business. The aristocratic French "industrial policy" advocate and the American Boy Scout "intellectual property" advocate could not have been more alien to one another.

Nevertheless, Boeing canceled its plans just three months after Airbus decided to go ahead with the A380 superjumbo project. Airbus had ignored an announcement from Boeing recommitting itself to the jumbo: the European firm had called Boeing's bluff. Airbus correctly guessed Boeing would not really take on the risks surrounding the launch of a stretch jumbo.[9]

There were two risks that kept Boeing from preempting Airbus's move into very large aircraft. Both show how skill differences in learnable risks complicate strategy.

First, Boeing couldn't be confident of Airbus's competitive response. It was unclear how well Airbus could design larger planes.

But it was even less clear that the European champion would feel much market pressure if Boeing preemption eroded the A380's economics. In fact, the complicated ownership and governance structure of Airbus made its sensitivity to the market much harder to predict than Boeing's.

Airbus, on the other hand, could reasonably well predict that shareholders would punish Boeing for a launch cannibalizing its flagship 747.[10] As a result, Boeing was less able than Airbus to estimate what share of the large aircraft market it might command.

Second, Boeing had reason to doubt how well it understood airlines' evolving needs and how they would respond to competing offerings. The popularity of the close similarity in cockpit design across all Airbus aircraft appears to have taken Boeing by surprise, for example. Boeing also had to wonder whether it could extrapolate the growth of point-to-point carriers like Southwest and congestion pressures on U.S. hub airports—both of which argued for smaller aircraft—to the burgeoning needs of Asia.

Airbus seemed to proceed with much greater confidence about the needs of Asian airlines and moved from success to success in that fast-growing market. In fact, the initial orders for the A380 included planes for both Qantas and Singapore Airlines.[11] Shortly after Airbus announced them, Boeing canceled the stretch jumbo for good.

The first two lines from a January 15, 2004, *Economist* article titled "Noël Forgeard, Airbus's Boeing-Beater" sum it up. "Phil Condit was forced to quit as boss of Boeing in November. Meanwhile, his counterpart since 1998 at Airbus, Noël Forgeard, goes from strength to strength." Condit was a victim of the fact that Airbus was, at least momentarily, in a better position to assess crucial business risks.

The challenges Boeing faced in estimating its likely share of a new market and in gauging the new needs of international airlines illustrate the cost of haziness about risk drivers. In the first case, uncertainty around market share made it hard to estimate the expected benefits of launching its stretch jumbo. In the second case, uncertainty around the developing needs of the world's airlines made it hard to gauge how misleading its experience might be.

Every learnable risk poses these two kinds of challenges, whether it's as weighty as the next decade's demand for air travel or as humble as the dependability of an office supply provider. Uncertainty makes it hard to estimate the expected benefits of a project or acquisition, process improvement or adaptive move. It might even lead us to assume that a project will be profitable when we should have expected it to lose money. If we can't be sure of the benefits, we can't be sure how much or even whether to invest.

But uncertainty about our uncertainty is in some ways worse. We become unsure of the inaccuracy in *any* result our experience generates and unclear about the margins for error we need to allow. The practical challenge this raises takes many forms. It may take the form of extra capital we must put up to absorb worse than worst-case losses. It may take the form of extra spending on controls or hedges we need to incur. It may take the form of more expensive capital as investors balk at risk in our cash flow projections. In Boeing's case, it would probably have been a mix of all three.

We must scope out each major business risk we identify to know how much it may cost us. If we think others may estimate that cost more accurately, we may want to avoid the risk altogether. The consequence is profound. Our *risk assessment ability* becomes a critical skill that can determine success.

VALUE AT RISK: AN UNCERTAIN MEASURE OF UNCERTAINTY

The possibility that this assessment skill could determine our success in a risky project is why we must start separating learnable and random risks. By definition, different people and different organizations have different information assets and levels of aptitude for assessing any new class of learnable risks. But that means some people and organizations may develop a competitive advantage in assessing those risks. With random risks, no one could have a scoping advantage, or the risks would be learnable.

This is an incredible conclusion. If you believe it, you must throw away your confidence that rewards will usually be proportional to learnable risks. After all, if someone else has an advantage in assessing some learnable risk, and the quality of that assessment makes a practical difference in business results, then we might *never* earn a fair return on the risk. Since the conclusion is startling, and since it depends on the notion of assessing a risk, we had better be clear about what we actually measure when we assess a risk.

The risk in buying a house can serve as an example. Many risks resemble house buying in mixing learnable and random sources of uncertainty. Housing prices are not as random as stock prices, because the housing market is less transparent, and listings information is incomplete. The housing market also seems subject to bubbles, which may be lifting housing prices in the United States and several European countries at the time of this writing. Mortgages involve random interest rate risks, however, raising the question of why we keep trying to "time" the mortgage market.

Our assessment of the risk in buying a house is just a casual version of what securities traders do to assess the risk in their trading positions. In both cases, there are basically two steps. First we estimate our exposure to what drives the risk, usually called the *risk factor:* we calculate the gains or losses that would result from different risk factor outcomes. Then we assess the variability of the outcomes of the risk factor itself. Knowing both of these things—how we stand to gain or lose from the risk factor and how the risk factor varies— lets us reckon our odds of gains and losses.

In the case of buying a house, for example, the first step is estimating our exposure to housing price swings. Suppose the housing market drops 2 percent this year and the price of our house drops with it. What is our exposure? The answer depends on our expectations.

If recent history suggested that housing prices in our particular market were growing 8 percent per year, then the 2 percent loss reflects a 10 percent disappointment, and we would multiply that 10 percent by the price we paid for the house. The resulting exposure is a dollar figure reflecting our loss (compared with what we expected) in one scenario for our housing price risk factor. We could repeat it for as many housing price scenarios as we like, or even for all of them if we want to graph it.

The second step is to understand the variability of the risk factor—namely, prices in the housing market. A realtor's data might show that the annual growth of housing prices has fallen within, say, 6 percent of average half the time and deviated more than 6 percent from average half the time. So there's nothing too surprising about a 6 percent drop from the price we expect for the house in a year's time. We must be prepared for such a drop. We would conclude that at least 6 percent of the cost of the house is at risk. With enough data, we could figure out the likelihood of any dollar gain or loss.

The example shows that when we put these two steps together—when we know how we stand to gain or lose from a risk factor and how the risk factor varies—we can determine a worst-case loss scenario for any level of comfort. For example, from the information given we can say the price of our house will fall more than 6 percent below expectations just 25 percent of the time. (It will also rise more than 6 percent above expectations 25 percent of the time.) Another way to put this is that 75 percent of the time the price will *not* fall more than 6 percent below expectations.

This is nothing more than a way of scoping a risk's worst-case loss, sometimes called the *value at risk*.[12] If our house costs $100,000, for example, then the worst-case loss at a 75 percent level of comfort is $6,000. A higher level of comfort would yield a larger worst-case loss, since it focuses on more extreme deviations.

In sum, knowing how we stand to gain or lose from a risk factor and how the risk factor varies lets us reckon a worst-case loss in dollar (or euro or yen) terms for any level of comfort. It's a way to scope or assess the losses threatened by a risk. Quantifiable risks are not the only ones where the difference between being learnable and random matters (see "Job Interviews and Hiring Risks That Are Hard to Measure"). But they often throw learning advantages into sharp relief, as we will see in the case of Nokia.

NOKIA, AIG, AND RISKS THAT DON'T "AVERAGE OUT"

Armed with a measure of risk, we can start to see how permanent winners and losers can arise in areas subject to learnable risks. What distinguishes a learnable risk is that we may be in a position to learn more or less about what drives it than other people or organizations confronting the same risk. The concept of value at risk suggests this will matter if it's costly to underestimate or overestimate our worst-case loss from the risk.

This is different from saying we may be better or worse than others at *managing* a risk. Of course we may. Our ability to manage a class of risks is part of our general management skill set. That skill set puts us at myriad small advantages and disadvantages that change constantly as our management practices change.

But it's another thing altogether to say that some people or organizations may be better than others at *assessing* a class of risks. An advantage in assessing a risk means you have better raw material in the form of information for managing it. That advantage will persist even as your complex of management practices changes over time. And a persistent advantage will lead to higher returns for taking the risk—even though traditional risk analysis suggests that everyone's results should converge to some average. Thus permanent winners and losers may arise regardless of management skills.

For example, Finnish telecommunications firm Nokia's superior assessment of mobile phone supply chain risks in 2000 gave it an enduring competitive advantage over Swedish rival Ericsson.

Job Interviews and Hiring Risks That Are Hard to Measure

The distinction between random and learnable risks matters even if we cannot quantify them. It's especially striking in the case of hard-to-measure hiring risks.

Job interviews are imperfect tests of the match between a job opening and a job seeker. The risks for the job seeker are fairly obvious. But there are risks on the other side, too. One is hiring the wrong person. Another is missing a hidden talent.

Suppose you interview two people, Don and Diane. Although Don's interviews have been mediocre, he has an impressive résumé, and the buzz is that your firm will make him an offer if your interview goes well. Diane's interviews have been all over the map. The catch is that it's clear that the interview process flusters her. Interviewing skills are not necessary for the job, and for some reason no one wants to write her off.

Your interview with Don goes a little better than your interview with Diane. But something bothers you, and you figure out what it is on the way home. You realize you know something about Don that few other people do. You both spent time working for a market research company that provides critical reviews of client products to help reposition them, and it's been very hard for you to overcome that critical point of view since you took up a sales position with your current firm. You must fight yourself to believe wholeheartedly in what you're now selling. It has worked out, but you feel lucky. You worry that Don might not be as lucky as you.

It was clear from the start, on the other hand, that the interview process unnerved Diane. In fact, the only time she calmed down was when you asked her how she would pitch specific products. In retrospect, she was fine as long as she wasn't selling herself.

How, from the perspective of learnable and random risks, could we make sense of your ultimate decision to give Diane a chance but to recommend against Don? Don's case is straightforward: there was a learnable risk in hiring him, and you were in a privileged position to evaluate it. In fact, it's unlikely anyone else could evaluate that risk as well as you for the job in question. You're probably not allowing any unconscious biases to interfere, since you're really saying, be careful with anyone too much like me!

Diane's case is harder. It seems the one thing that undermined her performance was the nature of the interview process itself. In other words, the variation in her interview performance seemed to arise from the very process of observation. That made it totally unpredictable. Diane presents something very like a random risk. You may doubt whether your slightly favorable impression of Diane was right. But there's no reason to think anyone else has a better point of view.

Your identification of the risk in hiring Diane as random tells you there is little reason to worry about others coming to a different conclusion based on better information. There really isn't better information about Diane, at least not from interviews, and instincts will have to serve.

Your identification of the risk in hiring Don as learnable, however, leads to the question of who is in the best position to evaluate it. In this case, you were. So the distinction between learnable and random risks helps explain why you might have had a very good reason to choose the candidate with the weaker interview.

On March 17, a rare thunderstorm struck the Albuquerque, New Mexico, factory of a major chip supplier for both firms. The Phillips Electronics plant caught fire and lost eight trays of silicon wafers—enough supplies for thousands and thousands of phones. Smoke and water damaged much of the rest of its chip stock. Even though Nokia would survive the crisis, Ericsson would abandon the market.

When Nokia's event management system detected a supply disruption three days later, the supplier warned the company's components purchasing manager that there would be a one-week delay. But Phillips declined to let visitors into the facility. So Nokia increased delivery monitoring from weekly to daily. Once Nokia determined that the disruption would last for months, it took two further steps. It demanded priority capacity from other Phillips plants. At the same time, it secured commitments from other U.S. and Japanese suppliers, reconfiguring its products to accommodate differing chip designs.

Ericsson seemed to have a weaker grip on the risks it faced. It accepted the supplier's early assurances and took no further action until April. But even then, Ericsson had little recourse. The firm had made a decision in prior years to cut costs through single-source contracts. It had no backups like Nokia's.

The disruption cost Ericsson €400 million in new sales and led it to discontinue mobile phone manufacturing. Nokia held production steady.[13]

Some said Nokia just had a greater drive to succeed in mobile phones than Ericsson. But if anything, Ericsson had a harder-driving culture. The firm changed CEOs three times between 1999 and 2003.

On the other hand, Nokia's CEO, Jorma Ollila, sounds like a sociologist on the rare occasions he makes public statements. "Speaking with Finnish philosopher Esa Saarinen," reported the *Moscow Times* in 2005, "Ollila said he thinks people are more concerned about individual rights than taking responsibility for their actions and trying to have a positive influence on society."[14]

What really made a difference to the two firms' ability to recover was their understanding of risk. Nokia mistrusted the supply chain and had arranged multiple-source contracting. Ericsson apparently thought the cost advantages of single-source procurement outweighed the risk of a supply chain concentrated in one provider.[15] Ericsson exited from the market because Nokia's risk assessment proved more accurate.

More specifically, Nokia had a better assessment of the risk of *concentrating* the chip supply chain for mobile phones than Ericsson. It must have projected a larger worst-case loss for a concentrated supply chain than Ericsson. That assessment probably would have secured market primacy for Nokia even if Ericsson had managed its risks better in all other respects. In other words, it was better risk assessment rather than ongoing risk management that vaulted Nokia to the top of the market.

Just as companies like Nokia have prospered in the face of new risks because they didn't *under*estimate them, plenty of companies have prospered under new risks because they didn't *over*estimate them. For example, property and casualty insurer AIG reestablished contact with China after the Cultural Revolution as early as 1980 and set up a joint venture with the People's Insurance Company of China (PICC). This was long before it was clear that Deng Xiaoping's reforms would succeed. In fact, he had been in power only two years at the time, and appeared to be reducing his own authority by resigning as vice premier. No other western insurer was active in the country.

But AIG had a history in China going back to 1919 that helped it judge the country's enormous commercial potential. The management team realized that even as China recovered from the Cultural Revolution, which had essentially died with Mao just four years earlier, it would not be long before an economic pragmatist like Deng unleashed market forces. AIG has maintained its leadership role in China ever since, acquiring 10 percent of PICC stock in October 2003 and getting access to its 121,000 sales representatives.[16] That's a platform if there ever was one.

Whether it's avoiding underestimates or overestimates of risk, examples like Nokia and AIG show how businesses can turn their information assets and knowledge into superior risk assessments that let them build winning positions.

But if that's right, it's the accuracy of the *worst-case loss estimates* made for a new risk that explains these successes. After all, worst-case loss estimates are what risk assessments assess. So the reason why differences in learnable risk assessments can have persistent consequences is that they lead firms to manage around radically different worst-case loss estimates for those risks.

This can't be the case with random risks. Since random processes drive random risks, no one knows better than anyone else what to expect. For example, most equity fund manager studies show that while some stock pickers have lucky streaks, even strong recent performers have no better chance than anyone else of beating the market going forward.[17] History is the best and only guide to the variability of random risk factors, and no one player has any privileged knowledge of whether history will change.

Learnable risks are risky, on the other hand, precisely because we lack information about their drivers. That information may be expensive, like climate data sufficiently detailed to support sharper short-term weather forecasts. Or we may simply lack good explanatory models for a risk, as when differences in accident rates persist among similar factories. Either way, different people or organizations may have very different bases for assessing a class of learnable risks. When they do, the differences in the assumptions on which they base their plans may persist.

THE BRAVE NEW WORLD OF
RISK-BASED COMPETITIVE ADVANTAGE

This distinguishing feature of learnable risks has the dramatic effect of adding a competitive dimension to how we need to think about them. But how can the variability of assumptions about a risk give rise to a competitive issue?

These assumptions have practical implications. In particular, they affect operating costs. Suppose Ericsson had been right about supply chain risk in the new mobile phone chip market, for example, and Nokia had been wrong. Then the lower cost base Ericsson derived from single-source procurement would have provided it with an ongoing cost advantage in its struggle with the Finns.

More important, persistent differences in risk assumptions may lead to a *sustained* difference in relative costs. One way of coping with risk is to hold extra capital to absorb losses. If somebody overestimates a risk, she will raise more capital than necessary and will have to cover the cost of that extra capital. Another way of coping with risk is to implement controls. If somebody overestimates a risk in this case, he may find himself spending more on those controls than necessary. A third way is to hedge the risk. But it can be expensive, and overhedging will drag down profits. In each case, the cost of an inferior risk assessment will persist. It will lead to an ongoing *relative* cost disadvantage.

The idea of relative cost has become so ingrained in our practical business thinking that we don't even notice it. It's not the absolute cost of a business process like, say, sales that matters. It's the relative cost that matters.

To see how ingrained the idea of relative cost has become, imagine a neighbor drops by with a business idea. He shoves a copy of the *Daily Trombone* through the kitchen door with a survey on the biggest unmet need in the county. Say it's figuring out what package of telephone, TV, and Internet services to get and how to set it up.

You would never reply, "Great idea, Frank, but think how much those systems cost!" The *absolute* cost of the business or its parts and material doesn't matter, at least not if it's a viable product or service. But you might well ask, "Gee, Frank, do you think we could do it any more efficiently than the women down the street? As you know, they started a business last Thursday doing exactly this, and they may have a cost advantage." The mind turns first to disadvantages in *relative* cost, and with reason.

Relative cost has been the focus of business planning since the 1970s, and it was codified in Michael Porter's book *Competitive Strategy.* Look at these lines from his second chapter.

Having a low-cost position yields the firm above-average returns in its industry despite the presence of strong competitive forces. Its cost position gives the firm a defense against rivalry from competitors, because its lower costs mean that it can still earn returns after its competitors have competed away their profits through rivalry. A low-cost position defends the firm against powerful buyers because buyers can exert power only to drive down prices to the level of the next most efficient competitor. Low cost provides a defense against powerful suppliers by providing more flexibility to cope with input cost increases . . . Thus a low-cost position protects the firm against all . . . competitive forces because bargaining can only continue to erode profits until those of the next most efficient competitor are eliminated, and because the less efficient competitors will suffer first in the face of competitive pressures.[18]

It's the cost position of a business relative to competing businesses that determines its profitability. Relative cost drives not only its success against competitors, in fact, but its leverage with customers and suppliers.

So why, given three decades of clear thinking about the importance of relative cost to business success, do we always focus on the absolute amount of risk in our projects? Why don't we focus on the relative strength of our ability to assess new risks, at least if they're learnable?

Imagine you've just started a home communications and entertainment service in your county. Your neighbor and business partner, Lisa, knocks on the back door and says, "The cable and telephone packages are fine, but I don't like the broadband data deals we're finding. Why don't we start our own wireless service?"

You might reply that she's right about the broadband deals, but it just sounds too risky getting that far in front of the market. In other words, we instinctively start thinking about the absolute level of risk in the business. Few, if any, of us would say the question is making sure we knew more about the market than anyone else.

Of course, absolute levels of risk matter. There are plenty of new ideas out there whose risks dwarf their potential rewards and should not be pursued. But if one of those new ideas is viable, it will *have* to produce benefits greater than at least one provider's predictable and risk-related costs. So for viable ideas, the issue really should be who can best size up the risks and determine the most efficient way to manage them.

Near the very beginning of his classic book, Porter explains why advantages in relative cost can create lasting success.

> *If costs decline with experience in an industry, and if the experience can be kept proprietary by established firms, then this effect leads to an entry barrier. Newly started firms, with no experience, will have inherently higher costs than established firms and must bear heavy start-up losses from below- or near-cost pricing to gain the experience to achieve cost parity with established firms (if they ever can) . . . If costs continue to decline with volume even as cumulative volume gets very large, new entrants may never catch up.*[19]

Porter's not talking about risk, here, but he could be. He's saying that if experience lets one company operate at lower cost than others in its business, that company may be able to stay ahead of its competitors and extract more profit from the business. It depends on whether experience continues to make a difference over time and how much the competitors are willing to spend to catch up.

Since risk has become an important element in any careful analysis of cost, we must extend Porter's ideas on relative cost to risk, or at least to learnable risks. After all, if one person has a better sense than other people of the worst-case loss that could arise from some new class of learnable risks, then that person may have a long-term competitive advantage in projects exposed to them. In the case of business lines, for example, competitors that *over*estimate those risks will stay out. Competitors that *under*estimate those risks will be unprepared for the occasional losses they will suffer and will have to adjust or abandon their projects.

In sum, we should think about more than the absolute level of risk in any project, process improvement, or acquisition we're considering. If our plans involve a learnable new risk, then we should think about our relative skill—driven by our information assets and knowledge—in assessing it. Whoever has the best handle on this new risk has a good chance of scoping out the challenge it poses more accurately. That means running a lower-cost operation that can still deal with the risk's uncertainties.

IF YOU THOUGHT RANDOMNESS WAS BAD, TRY IGNORANCE

Learnable risks raise competitive issues. Random risks don't. This is why our whole approach to a risky project, process improvement, or acquisition should depend on what kind of major risks it has.

Random risks, such as risks driven by energy prices, are hard to manage because they're, well, random. But learnable risks pose the problem of not only managing variability from the risk but also learning as much and as quickly about that variability as anyone else. If you thought randomness was bad, try ignorance.

The reality of risk-based competition should raise real alarms in some companies. It means you can run into trouble even if you can manage a project with learnable risks as well as anyone else. But if your organization can't move down the learning curve for its major risks as fast as your competitors, you probably won't resource your effort as efficiently as they do. Once again, you either overprotect yourself, maybe with a slow and careful sales ramp, and risk falling behind; or you underprotect yourself, perhaps overcommitting sales resources to the product and risking financial trouble.

At the end of the day, you might just prefer to sell products that pose truly random risks for your company. That way, at least, you need not worry about competitors learning more about the market and production risks you both face than you do. (There may be plenty of competitive differences in risk management, but, as argued earlier, those differences are more changeable and malleable than fundamental differences in learning speed.) If, on the other hand you're committed to a product with learnable risks, you'll want to make sure you can learn as much about those risks as anyone else selling it.

Recognizing this is crucial in selecting the projects we want to launch given the risks those projects will force us to assess and manage. But it also helps us separate learnable and random risks in the first place.

At the beginning of the chapter, we identified random risks mainly as financial risks reflecting the variability of prices in "complete" or at least robust markets. Burton Malkiel defined such markets as those where prices take a random walk and blindfolded chimpanzees throwing darts at the *Wall Street Journal* will do as well as the experts.[20]

The next step would be to determine which nonfinancial risks are also random. But telling which nonfinancial risks are truly random threatens to turn into an endless metaphysical exercise. The competitive challenge posed by learnable risks, however, suggests a quick, simple, and very pragmatic solution.

If the major class of risks underlying a new project seems unrelated to the random movements of some security, commodity, or derivative price, it probably makes sense to assume the risks are learnable. In other words, if no market is driving a risk, we can probably hope to learn *something* about its variability.

The reason is that that's the safer mistake to make. Think of it this way. If you assume some *learnable* risk is *random*, then you won't worry about whether someone else may learn more about the worst-case loss that could result from it than you can. But someone else may in fact get a better handle on that risk, and you may find yourself unable to break even on a project that bears it.

Now assume some *random* risk is *learnable*. The worst that can happen is that you will worry needlessly about how quickly other people or firms competing in business lines exposed to the same risk are learning about it. That's not so bad. Remember the advice of Intel CEO Andy Grove: "Only the paranoid survive."[21]

If you are in doubt about whether a risk is learnable or random, assume it is learnable. That way, you will pay attention to what you can learn about it and won't inadvertently overprotect or underprotect yourself from it, compared with a better informed competitor. In fact, "Randomness and Intimacy" suggests that risks reflecting market prices may be the *only* random ones you're likely to encounter.

WHY NOW?

To sum up, if the skills various people and organizations bring to bear on assessing a learnable risk vary, a basic assumption about risk measurement must change. The assumption that the worst-case loss you measure depends only on your exposure is wrong. It also depends on what you know and who else is taking the risk.

This in turn changes our fundamental assumptions about risk and reward. If people make different assumptions about worst-case losses from a risk, then they will spend different amounts controlling it, mitigating it, transferring it, or providing for losses from it. As a result, the returns they extract, even from identical projects, will vary.

And this changes our fundamental assumptions about the total *portfolio* of risks we bear across our projects, whether at home or at work. Instead of benefiting from how risks cancel each other out,

Randomness and Intimacy

The pragmatic rule of thumb that risks are learnable unless they arise from competitive market pricing may not be so far from the truth. It's actually related to the idea that randomness comes from self-reference.

Karl Popper tackled randomness using self-reference in *The Open Universe*.[22] He describes a thought experiment that tries to disprove determinism defined as predictability. The gist of the thought experiment is that a predicting machine cannot foretell its own future state of knowledge. To do so, it would have to calculate the prediction faster than it could develop the future knowledge to be predicted.[23]

Another version of the argument is that the machine could not finish its prediction, because it could not finish reading a full description of itself. The description would have to include a quote of the description, which would have to include a quote of a quote of the description, and so on. An intuitive version of the argument is that if we could predict our own future knowledge, it would no longer be future knowledge.

Popper also believed that at least some events have no determinate cause. In the language of this chapter, some things are random. But he argues that we cannot test this view (or its opposite).[24] So although he gives good reasons for randomness, he proves only the impossibility of self-prediction. That doesn't detract from his argument. But for our purposes, it strongly indicates that self-reference plays a special role in randomness.

It's as if predictability fails when we have too much information—namely, information about ourselves. This is true of the three clearest examples of randomness in economics, psychology, and physics. The problem with predicting prices in perfect markets is that those

(*continued*)

prices already incorporate all available information. The problem with self-analysis in psychology is that at some level we know too much. Physics fails to predict quantum states when, to measure them, the observer must overwhelm them in the sense of interfering with them.

This way of thinking about predictability may help clarify the connection between self-reference and pricing, and specifically pricing that follows Malkiel's random walk. The pricing mechanism in a competitive market sums up the perspective of every buyer, seller, or just plain shopper in it. For any good, there's only one market price. It arises from the market's self-interrogation about value. Competitive prices, in other words, are the outcome of a competitive market's self-referential computation.

It's worth noticing that complex and chaotic processes are generally not random. Information theory defines the complexity of a process as the length of the shortest computer program that can produce it, and randomness as cases where no such program is "shorter" than the process. But chaotic processes are often compactly described.[25] So even complex and chaotic risks can be learnable.

Another approach to randomness holds that we're forced to think of things outside our control in terms of external causes. But when it comes to what we affect, ourselves included, we are no longer forced to think in terms of external causes, and so we don't.

In this view, random risks are intimate: they arise from markets in which we're participating. Learnable risks, ironically, are more remote. That gets it about right. Learnable risks are the real unknown. Random ones are just unpredictable.

we could find ourselves pursuing a pack of losing propositions where someone, somewhere, knows more about the risks behind every one.

The bottom line is that learnable risks—including most, if not all, of the nonfinancial risks we face—just don't behave like random risks. How banks manage financial risks tells us very little about how we should approach our own risks—and not just because banks have more data! Much of what banks do benefits from the fact that so many of their risks are random. No one can know anything more about them than anyone else does. Track risk factor outcomes; understand your exposure; calculate worst-case losses. It does not matter who else faces the risk. Point and shoot.

But if learnable risks are so radically different from random ones, why are we just starting to notice the difference? Have learnable risks suddenly dropped down from Mars? Are they new? Have they somehow materialized out of nowhere?

Learnable risks can't be new, because nonfinancial business risks have always been with us. They may be starting to matter because of two big changes in our working and personal lives. First, as discussed in chapter 1, information technology is making it possible to manage business, and therefore learnable, risks more closely. Second, as a result, what we spend on managing learnable risks is growing to the point of rivaling other information costs. If this last point is right, it gets even clearer why it's becoming so important to separate learnable from random risks.

So why does a cost like that of handling a type of risk grow suddenly in importance? Of course, costs differ from one organization to another, from one division in a company to another, and even from one person to another. For example, one company will manufacture wheels more efficiently than another, one division in a company will collect its receivables faster than another, and one person will shovel snow from a driveway faster than another.

And yet at any point in time, these cost differences tend to be related. There is often a common source of the biggest differences in cost. During the industrial revolution, for example, differences in the cost of extracting and transporting commodities like iron ore tended to account for the biggest differences in primary-metals firms. But over time, commodity markets developed and better practices emerged that flattened materials costs across different companies.[26]

In much of the twentieth century, differences in labor costs dominated the cost structures of international manufacturing firms and drove global trade patterns. Thanks to the reemergence of floating exchange rates in the 1970s, though, labor prices have tended to adjust rapidly to productivity, to the point that it's hard to guess what manufactures some countries will be exporting to others. Differences in the absolute cost of labor remain, but the relation between labor cost and productivity has tended to be more and more stable across world markets in areas exposed to trade.[27]

As Japanese firms increasingly challenged western firms in the 1980s, differences in cost of capital became a dominant driver of differences in cost structure. Once international investment flows recovered from the inflation of the 1970s, however, these differences narrowed dramatically, and costs of capital have largely converged for financial instruments like long-term bonds.[28]

More recently, development economists led by Paul Romer have pointed to differences in the cost of information reflected in access to ideas as one of the most important explanations of development success and failure.[29] Romer has argued that only systematic differences in *know-how* can explain persistent differences in economic growth. It's as if the more the costs of material, labor (relative to productivity), and capital equalize across companies under more open international competition, the greater the importance of differences in information costs becomes.

Access to ideas is a principal driver of information costs in any organization. But another is the cost of handling uncertainty. It's too early to tell how much of any company's costs really come from handling uncertainty, because companies are only beginning to figure out how much of what they do is due to uncertainty. But the possibility that the cost of risk now lies on the "cost frontier" of the modern company explains why our efforts to get clear about business risks, including whether they are learnable or random, will repay us more than ever before.

In retrospect, this is the question my friend in the equipment manufacturing division wishes he could answer. He worries that his firm is not as well positioned to judge the risks in its business as are some of its competitors. What he really needs is a way to rate his firm's ability to grapple with those risks. He needs some kind of comparative intelligence score for risk.

3

Scoring Your Risk Intelligence (or Risk IQ)

So far as you have a choice among risky initiatives at work or projects at home—initiatives and projects with uncertain costs and outcomes—can the risks help you choose? The last chapter showed that the impact of information technology on our ability to assess learnable risks may create permanent winners and losers in business. Who wins depends on risk skills. Some learnable risks just aren't fair bets for some of us. How bad are those bets?

Maybe the reason people haven't paid much attention to what's different about learnable risks has been the dearth of good ideas for measuring our learning skills. But we *can* measure our ability to learn about risks. Even if we can only roughly compare our ability to learn about a type of risk with others', we may make vastly better risk decisions and project choices. This chapter provides a simple method to tell whether you are more likely to win or lose with the various learnable risks of your potential projects.

This is a new idea. We have long known that some people are better than others at *managing* risks. We've measured those management skills as we measure all management skills—with great difficulty. But everything changes if we can start to measure our skill in *assessing* different kinds of learnable risks.

We may find we can measure this ability for any given learnable risk more objectively than we can measure most management skills.

We may find the ability of people and organizations to assess any class of these risks differs more predictably than most management skills (which are so hard to pin down that many management scientists label them an "art" defying further analysis).

We may find our ability to assess different learnable risks varies more widely than our other skills in managing them.

And we may improve our own long-term performance if we compare our assessment skills with others on a risk-by-risk basis.

So this chapter's goal is to implement the second rule of risk intelligence:

Rule 1. Recognize which risks are learnable.

Rule 2. Identify risks you can learn about fastest.

WHY RISK ASSESSMENT SKILLS MATTER

It may seem incredible that measuring a skill could make much of a difference to our success in business, at work, at home, in our private lives, or in raising children. After all, there are plenty of skills we could measure without making any practical difference in our lives. For example, our skill in judging character bears strongly on how we raise children. But it's hard to imagine that an ability to measure that skill would make a difference in how we run our families.

The difference is that while we can't "choose" who our children are, we can and do exercise freedom in selecting the risks we bear. It's because we make free choices of which risks to bear (in the form of choices among projects, acquisitions, time allocations, and so forth) that an ability to measure our risk assessment skills can make a material difference in our ability to succeed.

A friend in town who works for a Washington, D.C., public relations firm doesn't think she chose her risks last year. She lost a print media account because of an unedited wardrobe malfunction in a photograph, her Internet initiative tanked, and then her mother needed a hip replacement. "I wasn't in control of any of that," she says.

Maybe not, but we have a lot more choice than this example suggests on the surface. Say a proofreader misses one still photo in a project involving hundreds of similar ones. Suppose the proofreader was not a normal hire but rather someone brought in to do creative work from another firm. In this case, the choice was to take a risk on an unusual hiring method. Moreover, it was a risk that others in the recruiting department may have understood better. However uncontrollable operating risks like proofreading errors may seem to be, there is often a free choice at the root of them.

The reason we have a choice as to which risks we take is that we have a choice as to which projects we will pursue, how we will spend our time, and what things we want to improve in our businesses and our homes. All these choices imply different risks. It only makes sense to consider the risks in making the choices.

What's new is the idea that our ability *relative to others* to understand and learn what drives a risk could make or break a project bearing that risk. There are growing differences in how much and how quickly people and organizations can learn about many risks. So our ability to measure our relative skill in assessing them becomes vital.

In 2001, for example, a lot of companies around the country started investing in fiber-optic cable, exposing themselves to new risks. Differences in their ability to evaluate those risks became clear when the telecommunications bubble burst.

The Tulsa, Oklahoma–based Williams Companies, an energy sector conglomerate that sells and distributes natural gas and petroleum, was one of these investors. Looking to expand its revenue stream, the executives at Williams decided to launch a fiber-optic subsidiary called Williams Communications Group. But its relative inexperience with fiber-optic risks would prove more important than its property right advantages in determining success or failure.

At first it seemed like a logical venture since Williams already had the rights to thousands of miles of pipeline. So it could assure stockholders like Intel Corporation and SBC Communications that it could minimize risk by laying telecommunications cable along those same pipeline routes. But an energy company like Williams had less experience than telecommunications firms in judging the risk of a glut in the market.

It didn't take long for the fiber-optic market to nose-dive after so many companies laid so many miles of optical cable in the ground. The stock price of Williams's subsidiary dropped in 2001 from $61 to 67¢. Some shareholders brought a lawsuit against Williams arguing that company executives were touting the value of their fiber-optic network at a time when "more than enough miles of optical fiber to reach the sun were laid around the world."

The concept of relative risk assessment skills might have led Williams to ask whether it could interpret changing fiber-optic business conditions as well as its more experienced competitors. A difference in risk assessment made a difference in outcomes.

A great example of winning by assessing risk better than everyone else is the case study of the Oakland A's baseball team that Michael Lewis describes in his book *Moneyball.* In fact, Oakland's general manager, Billy Beane, explicitly devours baseball statistics to get an edge on his competitors in shaping his team.

One of baseball's biggest risks, let alone mysteries, is player performance. It's a serious problem for general managers like Beane in smaller or two-team cities that just don't have the money to buy all the talent they can find. The smartest thing Beane could have done was to master the risks driving player performance better than his competitors.

Beane realized that baseball generates mounds of statistics. It should be possible to learn almost anything about the game from them. So why did all the other managers blindly bid for players with high batting averages and pitchers with low earned-run averages? In all those statistics pouring out of every game, there must be better clues to what makes a championship team.

Beane found some. He started looking for players with high on-base averages, whether they batted themselves onto the field or walked, and pitchers who coaxed a lot of groundouts. These players often lacked the marquee statistics other teams sought, so he picked them up on the cheap. The result has been the rags-to-riches story of a contender in recent playoffs. You could not find a clearer story of winning on risk.

Of course, risk managers have always known that skill matters. But they had no way to measure the kind of skill—the learning capacity—that separates successful risk takers from the ones who end up scratching their heads. On the other hand, there are plenty of measures that show how much new risks diversify your total exposure. It's a dangerous combination because it encourages us to brave new risks even if we have no hope of mastering them. Since most people manage what they can measure, the lack of a risk skill metric, combined with an abundance of risk diversification metrics, has pushed us beyond what we're good at doing.

MEASURING RISK INTELLIGENCE

Put simply, we need a test to measure our ability to assess learnable risks. More exactly, we need a way to score learning speed relative to others grappling with the same learnable risk. The simplest test equal to the challenge consists of five elements measuring the impact that your experiences in business, job, or outside life are likely to have on your ability to reach accurate judgments about a specific new risk. Structured like the widespread Apgar score used to gauge the health of newborn babies, this test regarding the risks of embryonic projects lets you quickly assess your relative ability to assess a new risk, or even old ones that are giving you concern. Let's define *risk intelligence* ("risk IQ") as both intelligence about a risk and a result of the score.

For each of the five elements, give yourself a 2 if your experiences or your firm's business interactions—here called "experiential tests"—put you in a better position than others to reach accurate judgments. Give yourself a 1 if there's no reason to think you're different, and a 0 if you think others may do better. Scores fall from 0 to 10; 5 is average.

You can actually rank your projects by your learning scores for their major risks to determine how effectively you are likely to manage each one to a gain over time. Of course, lots of factors drive risk management. What this test picks out is your relative ability to gauge the main risks to react to them.

You should avoid projects with risks on which you give yourself the lowest scores. But since that's not always possible, the question is what you can do to improve your risk IQ, at least for a specific type of risk. The score's five-part framework (see table 3-1) provides a road map for improving it with respect to any learnable risk.

To illustrate how this test works, let's use an example from the real estate business. Every prospective agent takes a risk in deciding where to focus—on what residential area in a city, for example, or on

TABLE 3-1

Risk intelligence score

How often do you have experiences related to the risk?	
How relevant are these experiences to what might influence the risk?	
How surprising are these experiences?	
How diverse are these experiences as sources of information?	
How methodically do you keep track of what you learn from them?	
Total	

what type of residential or commercial buildings. Agents often have a terrible time moving from one market to another or from one kind of property to another within the same market. But agents can determine how well positioned they are to handle the risks of a new real estate market by taking this test. Let's go through an example of what a residential real estate agent in Los Angeles (LA) should ask himself in considering a move into smaller commercial properties.

First, it's necessary to determine what the principal risk behind the decision is. To keep the example simple, let's assume the main risk involves the kind of commercial properties small businesses will need in the current economy.

1. *How frequently do your experiences relate to the risk?* How often do you meet people or hear arguments providing insight into the kind of businesses that are expanding in LA at the moment? There's no need to answer in the abstract. In fact, the question is meaningful only relative to other commercial agents. Think of it in terms of "exposures per week." Score yourself a 2 if you think you have more exposure to these insights on a week-to-week basis than most agents. Give yourself a 1 if you think the number of times you are learning something about commercial property needs each week is about average. Mark a 0 if you think others have an edge.

2. *How relevant are these experiences to what might influence the risk?* What's the range of implications of your typical experience regarding LA business expansion for different factors that might influence the area's commercial property needs? Say you found rapid price growth near an expanding film studio on a new subway line and flat prices around a very similar studio far from the subway. This suggests it's unlikely that studio growth drives much nearby property activity but very possible that subway line extension is having

an effect. So the experience or finding has a wide range of implications for different possible factors: from unlikely to very possible. This crucial question asks whether your typical experience helps you rule out factors that don't matter and focus on those that may. You can make it concrete by estimating the proportion of your experiences that are both 100 percent likely if some factors are in fact driving the market and 100 percent impossible if other factors were driving it. Give yourself a 2 if you may have more of these "yes or no" experiences than other commercial agents, a 1 if you are average, and a 0 if others may have an edge.

3. *How surprising are these experiences?* How unexpected is what you learn from your typical exposure to information about LA business expansion? The more surprising the experience, the more it tells you about factors behind the area's commercial property needs. In other words, when something unusual happens, you really must pay attention. This is really a measure of the improbability of your experiences. It probably won't change your views to learn, for example, that properties on street corners do well. The observation was expected. But you may be very surprised to see how quickly an old 1950s dance hall with a wide-open space on its second floor moves. Score yourself a 2, 1, or 0 based on whether you suspect your typical experiences are unearthing more unexpected or improbable news than those of other commercial agents.

4. *How diverse are these experiences as sources of information?* Do you engage in a variety of activities that could make you a better commercial agent? For example, do you visit lots of different kinds of retail shops? Do you have any friends in warehousing or manufacturing? Do you keep up with traffic and public transportation changes? Do you know any

developers, and do you follow the construction sector? This question focuses on the range of your information sources. The idea is that frequent exposure to data from the same sources may not tell you anything new. The important thing, as always, is how you compare with others. Again, give yourself a 2, 1, or 0.

5. *How methodically do you track what you learn?* Do you keep some kind of record of what you learn from the news and from your various contacts with builders, developers, clients, and other agents? For example, do you keep track of which properties sell and which ones don't? Do you keep a record of your own successes and failures, especially the startling surprises, and your sense of the reasons for them? The issue here is not backing up memory. It's enabling better organizational performance, especially if you're thinking of working with a team of agents. It's about keeping a record of how your beliefs have evolved with new information about the market. Give yourself a 2 if you think you keep track of what you learn more systematically than others, a 1 if you think you are average, or a 0 if you think others may have an edge.

Once you have the cumulative score, you should take three next steps.

- *Triage your risks.* First, compare your scores for the main risks underlying your projects and triage them. Just as a maternity ward uses the Apgar score developed decades ago to decide how to care for newborns, decide which risks you can handle best, and leave the rest to others.

- *Diagnose your risk intelligence.* Second, diagnose your risk intelligence scores to see if there is a systematic problem you can fix. Perhaps you cut yourself off from bad news and should seek out more relevant feedback. Or you may swamp yourself with conflicting data that gives little direction.

- *Classify yourself as a risk assessor.* Third, look over the components of your risk intelligence scores for patterns. What kind of risk assessor are you? Do you take in a lot of information but not necessarily the most telling kind? Do you learn a lot and then forget it?

Let's look at these three steps in turn, with a brief note of recognition for the inventor of the newborn health score on which I've based this measure of risk intelligence (see "Virginia Apgar").

TRIAGE YOUR RISKS

To start, list all your possible projects and decisions whose risks pose learning challenges. Then identify the most important risks in each. Finally, determine whether your risk intelligence scores are substantially higher for some of those project possibilities.

Major risks will often revolve around the size of the market for a new product or the difficulty of adapting new technologies. But they could equally relate to competitor reactions, our ability to find talent, or the complexity of a supply chain.

Our most important risks are the ones that make us worry. They are the risks that make our projections of future results and timelines least certain. They can lead to the largest worst-case losses or disappointments compared with expectations.

Why can we be confident that there are only a few major risks underlying any given project or decision? One reason is that risk intelligence scores are applicable only to learnable risks. But the general observation that in any problem there are only a *vital few* crucial-to-address challenges comes down to us from Vilfredo Pareto (see "Pareto's Analysis").

Virginia Apgar

Born in Westfield, New Jersey, in 1909, Virginia Apgar graduated from Columbia's College of Physicians and Surgeons in 1933 and in 1949 became the first woman appointed full professor there. She had specialized in the neglected but rapidly growing field of anesthesiology after colleagues discouraged her—as a woman—from trying to break into surgery, and focused in the 1950s on obstetrics.[1]

In 1952 she developed a simple five-factor, ten-point scale to help doctors and nurses evaluate the health of newborns. A mnemonic for the factors was later developed using the letters of her name: Appearance, Pulse, Grimace, Activity, and Respiration.

She also took a degree in public health at Johns Hopkins in 1959 and later headed the birth defects division of the March of Dimes. She loved, built, and played early musical instruments all her life and died in New York City in 1974.

The Apgar score for newborns is used around the world because of its simplicity. My wife, Ann Marie Moeller, encountered it in so remote a place as a maternity clinic in the village of Banamba, Mali. The sobering experience of a maternity clinic in a country as poor as Mali taught her that the score's full ten-point range is indeed used once you get outside the hospitals of the industrialized world.

Virginia Apgar's neonatal score is relevant here not just because it offers a simple model for risk intelligence scores or because of the curiosity of the distant family relation. It also illustrates a point about the subjectivity of scores. Any two nurses may score newborns differently. But there will probably be enough consistency in any nurse's application of the score to guide emergency care for that nurse's newborns.

To get a little more familiarity with the way risk intelligence scores work, let's break the comparison of risk intelligence for the major project or decision options you're considering into the score's elements. In other words, compare your scores across the risky project or decision alternatives you want to evaluate for each risk intelligence element in turn.

Frequency of related experiences

Once you have identified the main risks underlying your projects or decisions, it's straightforward to score yourself for each of those risks using the first element—how frequently you have related experiences. For example, do you have more marketing visits per week on a given subject than your competitors? If you're planning to enter the German market, how many people on your team are reading the German business press compared with other possible entrants? Do you see suppliers more often than other players in a new product area? If you're a military planner thinking about a door-to-door anti-insurgency campaign, do you have better or worse contact with local people than whoever you think is directing the insurgency? The goal is to determine where your frequency of related experiences gives you an advantage over competing risk takers.

Relevance of typical experience

The next two elements—how relevant is your typical experience to what may influence a risk and how surprising is it—form the core of the risk intelligence score. Together, they characterize not the number or range of experiences that bear on a risk but the value of a *typical* experience. That value depends jointly on the dimensions of relevance and surprise. Those dimensions capture how effectively your typical experience weeds out factors unimportant or irrelevant to thinking about the risk.

The relevance element rates how well your experiences typically discriminate among possible factors influencing each risk you're

Pareto's Analysis

Born in 1848 to an Italian nationalist marquis self-exiled in France, Vilfredo Pareto tried running the Rome railway and a steel plant in Florence before retiring in frustration to Fiesole, where he married the exotic Russian Alessandrina Bakunin and wrote neo-classical economic broadsides until the government sent thugs to shut him up. Riots in the 1890s left him a cynical pragmatist, convinced all ideologies were due to elites competing for power.

He moved to Switzerland and wrote a remarkable manual of political economy introducing general equilibrium theory and criticizing utilitarianism with his concept of Pareto optimality. In it, he reinterprets utilities merely as preferences rather than objective values and shows that markets can reach an optimal point where no one can become better off without hurting someone.

But Pareto is most famous for his observation that 20 percent of the population always seems to control 80 percent of the wealth. His statistical argument also implies that 20 percent of any effort will normally achieve 80 percent of the results. By the same token, 20 percent of the risks of any endeavor should generate 80 percent of its value at risk.[2] These risks are the *vital few* that we need to consider for each of our project or decision alternatives.

scoring. Less relevant experiences are consistent with a broad range of possible factors. For example, the failure to get a prospective client to accept a sales visit tells little about the value of, say, the news service you are pitching. Whether the truth is that the service is of great potential value to many clients or the concept is flawed, there's a good chance any given prospect will be too busy for a visit. So the experience, or lack of one, is not very relevant to the real value of the service.

Relevant experiences are *not* consistent with a broad range of possible factors. If a prospect who you thought would value the news service explains to you why it is redundant, the experience of the visit sharply discriminates between your hopes that the news service will sell widely and the reality that in at least some segments it won't. That may not be the result you hoped to achieve, but you learned a lot. It's the experiences that are *not* consistent with all the possible factors influencing a risk—that could rule out some of those factors— that help assess the risk.

The goal here is determining which of your project possibilities your experiences are most relevant to. Since the scores are calculated relative to other risk takers, though, you're really comparing the relevance of your experiences relative to the typical experiences of competing risk takers.

Surprise or memorability of typical experience

The surprise element complements the element of relevance in capturing the value of a typical experience for understanding whatever risks you're triaging. Surprising or unexpected experiences tell us more about the world. If just 5 percent of your sales calls convert, you learn more about what you're selling from the prospect who converts than from those who don't. If you're evaluating an auto repair shop, you will learn most by talking to the rare customer whose car the shop couldn't fix.

This raises a possible confusion about the surprise element. How can your *average* experience be surprising? Surely it must simply be average. But that's not really true of our experiences. Sometimes we learn more than at other times and sometimes our experiences are truly extraordinary.

Think of a time when you were rapidly learning some new skill on the job or subject at school. Perhaps you had just switched jobs and were learning how to deal with a new set of colleagues in a new office culture. During that period, you probably had more surprising or unexpected experiences each day than during most other periods of time you spent on the job. They may have involved unexpected personality traits around you and ways to navigate around them. They may have involved new kinds of problems that forced you to learn new methods or solution strategies. Or they may have involved new demands on you for running meetings or presenting yourself.

Think of another time when you had an experience that made a deep impression on you. Perhaps you experienced a striking act of kindness. Or you may have witnessed unusually complex decision making during a boardroom presentation. What matters for the surprise element of a risk intelligence score, at any rate, is its improbability.

In evaluating what our typical experiences tell us about a specific kind of risk, this element of surprise matters especially in conjunction with the element of relevance. Surprising experiences greatly narrow the possibilities, or else they wouldn't be surprises. Experiences that are relevant to what may influence a risk have the *potential* to rule out many factors that don't really matter and that we can ignore. When a relevant experience is also surprising, it actually *does* rule out a lot of factors we might wrongly have taken as critical in learning to negotiate the risk.

For example, suppose we're comparing the ability of an antique dealer I know, my neighbor at the Federal Reserve Board, and me to predict silver prices. (I'm assuming for the moment that silver markets are not perfectly competitive, but that may not be true.) I have a lot of related experiences that are surprising because I read a lot of economic "tales of the weird." But those economic stories are not generally very relevant to the silver market. The antique dealer, on the other hand, has a lot of relevant experience in that she keeps an eye on prices for silver. But the price movements she watches casually rarely yield big surprises. Finally, my neighbor at the Fed has experiences that are both relevant and surprising on a regular basis. He actually looks for incidents around the world that will affect metals markets.

By now you've compared the scores for the relevance and surprise of your typical experiences with respect to the alternative risks you're considering. Together, those comparisons indicate which of your project or decision options bear risks that your typical experiences help you understand better than competing risk takers.

Diversity of experiences

Now compare the range or diversity of your experiences relating to each risk for which you're rating your assessment skills. The idea here is that variety is best. So if you have ten sales calls a week related to the risk in expanding your firm's Dallas plant but five sales calls and five supplier calls a week related to the risk in expanding your firm's St. Paul plant, you probably will be better at assessing the risk in St. Paul.

Record keeping

Finally, compare your diligence in tracking what you learn related to the key risks on which you're scoring yourself. Do you take notes in meetings? Do you create electronic records of important results and structure them so that others can understand what you've learned? For example, if you keep better records of employee health problems than supplier problems, then you may be better at projects with personnel risk than projects with supply chain risks.

How often should you triage your risks? The answer is, *exactly as needed.* That may seem jarring since financial institutions and investors reevaluate their risks regularly even if their exposure or positions *haven't* changed. Of course, they do so in case the probability distribution of an underlying risk factor *has* changed. They assume that if it has, they can change their investments or exposures. We rarely have the same discretion in our exposure to the business risk underlying a project we've accepted, however.

We should triage the major learnable risks we face every time we confront a possible choice among new projects, priorities, or risky alternatives. We face such choices when opportunities arise. We also face a risky choice when we *should* be looking for alternatives but neglect to do so. The risk in the latter case is that we might be resting on our laurels when we should be innovating and pursuing new opportunities.

So should we reevaluate our risk intelligence between new opportunities once a quarter, once a year, or irregularly on a yearly basis? It depends on when we master the risks underlying our current businesses and projects enough to have some capacity to undertake and learn about new ones. Chapter 4 develops the idea that our *learning capacity* is like a pipeline to be used fully and continuously but not overloaded.

DIAGNOSING AT&T'S RISK INTELLIGENCE: A MISMATCH BETWEEN RISKS AND SKILLS

To see how to apply these scores, let's evaluate AT&T's risk intelligence for three of the most important growth decisions it made in the years prior to its merger with SBC. They turned out to be missteps. Together, they weakened the company so much that one of the local "Baby Bell" companies spun off from AT&T in 1984 ended up buying it.

The first was the decision to put off—ultimately from 1984 to 1994—the pursuit of wireless telecommunications. The second was the failure in the two decades after the breakup of the company in 1984 to exploit its computing assets and create a position in broadband Internet technology. The third was the firm's late and abortive move into cable in the late 1990s. Table 3-2 proposes a rough evaluation of each element of AT&T's risk IQ for the business risks posed by wireless, broadband, and cable. Here, to keep things simple, a 2 means "high," a 1 "OK," and a 0 "low."

Where do numbers like these come from? One of the advantages of the risk intelligence score is that it can be as scientific as you have time

TABLE 3-2

AT&T's risk IQ for three tough decisions

	Wireless	Internet	Cable
Amount of experience	1	2	0
Relevance of experience	0	1	1
Surprise of experience	1	0	2
Diversity of experiences	0	1	1
Record keeping	2	1	0
Total	**4**	**5**	**4**

and resources to make it. But it sheds light on where we should be boldest in taking risks even without careful measurement. I wrote these numbers down sitting in an armchair with a review article in my hand from the *Economist* and a good casual knowledge of the company.[3] What this really shows is how much you can tell about an organization's capabilities when you marshal your facts in an effective way.

Wireless

Look at the scores in the first column of numbers. They characterize how well AT&T's experiences prepared it for risky decisions about getting into wireless starting in 1984. With the government-ordered breakup of the company fresh and most of its middle management intact, AT&T likely still enjoyed a huge advantage in institutional memory, reflected in a 2 for record keeping.

Glaring weaknesses included overreliance on a McKinsey study forecasting only 1 million wireless phone users by 2000—off by a factor of 740, as it turned out. That's why the firm gets a 0 for diversity of experiences as sources of information. It also gets a 0 for relevance or pertinence of experience since AT&T had little institutional basis to understand customer demand for portability. By the time the firm finally bought McCaw Cellular in 1994, it had to pay $11.5 billion, a price so high that its average growth over the next ten years until AT&T sold it would prove less than 14 percent.

Internet

By the 1990s, the company's strength in institutional memory had become a mixed blessing. AT&T failed to lever Western Electric's equipment business, the UNIX operating system it wrote in the 1970s, or its 1991 acquisition of NCR to shape computing, and divested the renamed Lucent in 1995. Famously, it shied away from operating the Internet backbone despite prodding by the Clinton administration. The company lacked any clear long-odds "win" in networked computing that might have shed light on the Internet's potential. The scores reflect this lack of a "basis for boldness" in a 0 for the surprise or memorability of its related experience.

What AT&T did have in spades was a ton of raw experience, reflected in a 2 for "amount." But that was not enough to put it in the lead of a market for broadband that now includes 30 percent of U.S. households.[4]

Cable

The risks, and therefore the story, change once again in the late 1990s as AT&T's new CEO, Michael Armstrong, bought cable giants TCI and Media One. The problem was that he bought them at the height of the market and could not drive cash flow to reduce debt fast enough. When telecommunications share prices collapsed in 2002, he had to give up on his dream of cable telephony.

Not only did AT&T's institutional memory fail again, apparently forgetting lessons about market timing from McCaw, but Armstrong also proved too new to cable competition to turn TCI around. So give the company a 0 for record keeping and amount of related experience. The fact that Ma Bell finally pulled the trigger and acquired a new technology, however, reflects its ability to put to work Armstrong's experience in achieving *unlikely* technological successes at Hughes Electronics and IBM earlier in his career. That justifies a 2 for the value of surprising or highly memorable experience. But it couldn't overcome AT&T's lack of executive and institutional cable experience overall.

AT&T's risk story

Even though they come from a casual armchair exercise, these scores for AT&T's risk intelligence in wireless in 1984, the Internet in the mid-1990s, and cable in the late 1990s tell a story. The scores for the company's ability to assess wireless and cable risks appear a little below average, but for very different reasons. Its reliance on a consulting study reflects the narrowness and limited relevance of its experience to the wireless business. This helps explain why AT&T delayed investing in the sector too long to compete effectively. Fifteen years later, a different set of disadvantages impaired its ability to pull off a late entry into cable. They included inexperience in managing cable's extreme revenue volatility and increasingly disrupted organizational memory.

Ironically, AT&T seemed as well positioned as others to stake out a role in broadband Internet services. While it was under pressure to get out of the equipment business, equipment would not prove central to Internet services. Here it seems that the company's lack of a galvanizing technology success led it to avoid a game it might have played well. If that shyness kept it from investing in broadband while Internet companies were still cheap, then this may have been AT&T's most tragic episode of all.

CLASSIFY YOURSELF AS A RISK ASSESSOR

Across three very different sets of business risks, twenty years, and numerous corporate transformations, AT&T's risk assessment profiles vary. But for most of us, and most of our organizations, we'll find highly consistent strengths and weaknesses in our ability to gauge even widely different business risks.

By comparing our own risk intelligence scores across the various projects, decisions, and improvement initiatives we are contemplating, we can see whether important patterns emerge. For example, three distinct patterns of scores—really patterns of strength and weakness in our organizational or personal learning—deserve special attention. They reveal blind spots that may obscure our vision across *all* our projects. There are straightforward ways to start rectifying all three.

The three patterns of risk assessment strengths and weaknesses are impressionists, encyclopedists, and amnesiacs. Briefly, *impressionists* anchor on highly memorable experiences that often lack relevance to their immediate problems. *Encyclopedists* accumulate a wealth of superficial knowledge that may have a bearing on real problems but lacks surprise and tells little that's not already known. *Amnesiacs* gather experience that's relevant and memorable. But they don't distinguish it from less important information and preserve it for ready use when needed. Let's flesh out the three types a little more and then do some troubleshooting.

Impressionists

Impressionists anchor on strong experiences and then apply them broadly. The problem is that they apply them too broadly. The memorability of their experiences is much greater than the relevance of their experiences.

What makes for a strong impression? The essential element of strong impressions or experiences is *improbability*. We don't really learn that much from experiences we expect. For example, we wouldn't learn much from hearing that an unpublished single mom who recently returned to Edinburgh from Portugal had written a midlist children's book. But our view of the children's book market changes permanently when we learn that J. K. Rowling sold over 3 million copies of *Harry Potter and the Sorcerer's Stone* in its first two years. Because the information is improbable, it makes a big impression on us. It is high-impact news, and we anchor on it.

Amos Tversky and Nobel laureate Daniel Kahneman identified the phenomenon of anchoring in 1979, in which decision makers focus on a formative experience and then overrely on it or even filter out contrary experiences. Gary Belsky and Thomas Gilovich later popularized the concept and warned about the bad decisions that arise from it.[5]

But despite decades of warnings about anchoring, improbable experiences have a strong impact on us for a very good reason. Surprising experiences tell us that something was wrong with our expectations. For example, the improbable ramp of *Harry Potter* shows that a children's book's first year need not be the crucial one (it sold 3 million copies in 1999 against 136,000 in 1998). Surprising experiences may not reveal the future. But they show us what's wrong with our view of the present.

Tversky and Kahneman never entirely explained when anchoring is a problem and when it isn't. But the impressionist pattern of risk intelligence does. The impressionist's highly memorable experiences are misleading when they are not *relevant* to a particular problem or the risks underlying it. If we tried to apply J. K. Rowling's experience to thrillers, for example, it might prove irrelevant despite the impression it made on us.

How can we test the relevance of a very memorable impression? The risk intelligence score shows how to measure the relevance of an experience to a set of risks. That measure is the sensitivity of the experience to different factors that might drive the risk. More precisely, it's the range of probabilities of the experience if different *possible* factors really applied. If our experience would have been unimaginable under some factors but a dead certainty given others, then the experience is relevant to determining what really drives the risk.

For example, suppose you work for a packaged food company, and your boss remembers spending a long time setting up a sales chain in India. Let's say it all fell through at the last moment because some official somewhere demanded a large bribe. It was a big disappointment after a lot of hard work. It was a surprise after a lot of early cooperation and honest dealings. Your boss anchors on the experience.

So now your boss is very reluctant to try to set up distributors in Vietnam. You and your team believe the main uncertainties *there* relate to security. If you're right, this would make your boss's experience irrelevant to Vietnam. None of the risk scenarios your team thinks may be true in Vietnam would make a last-minute request for a bribe more or less likely. So the experience tells little about which of the risk scenarios you're evaluating will probably hold for that country.

If, on the other hand, you were looking at a country where you had heard reports of bribery, then your boss's experience may be relevant. Some of the alternative possible risk scenarios you might envision for this country could make your boss's experience much more likely than others. For example, you could imagine a scenario where the local government keeps a tight lid on business dealings in the capital city but has limited control in remote cities. It's quite understandable how distributor negotiations could proceed smoothly in this scenario only to end up with a deal-killing demand for a bribe as you tried to secure arrangements farther from the capital. This situation would have led to just what happened to your boss. She was right to bring her "anchor" to the table in this business situation because her highly memorable experience was relevant to it.

It's precisely because improbable experiences make such a strong impression on us that we try to apply them where they are irrelevant. That's why Kahneman believes impressionists abound and that's why we must watch out for the pattern in ourselves. Do you rate your personal experience highly on surprise but not as highly on relevance for risk after risk? If so, you may be an impressionist.

In fact, that's what distinguishes impressionists in the first column of table 3-3. The columns give typical risk intelligence scores for three types of risk assessors. Focusing on the first column, you will see that impressionists are average in the amount and diversity of experience they bring to bear on their projects' risk problems. They are average in the thoroughness of their record keeping. But their experiences are typically strong in surprise while weak in relevance to most of the problems they face.

More specifically, their experience is richer than average in improbable or highly memorable learning. An example would be someone who sells large, complex systems, where each successful sale is quite unusual and therefore tells a lot about what drives customers' needs. Another would be someone like a merger adviser whose business dealings are unique, where every deal differs strikingly from the rest.

Similarly, the impressionist's experience is weaker than average in its relevance to different risks. This might be because it is restricted to a very narrow set of risk factors that don't apply widely to other business problems. Think of an industrial engineer focused closely on specific design failures, for example.

TABLE 3-3

Sample scoring for three risk intelligence patterns

	Impressionists	Encyclopedists	Amnesiacs
Amount of experience	1	1	2
Relevance of experience	0	2	1
Surprise of experience	2	0	1
Diversity of experiences	1	1	1
Record keeping	1	1	0
Total	5	5	5

So what can you do about it? Looking at the typical risk intelligence score for impressionists in table 3-3, you see that the big gap is in relevance. This, after all, is what undermines the potential of memorable experiences. How can impressionists enhance the relevance of their experience without sacrificing its memorability? The three most important practical steps impressionists can take fall under three of the elements of the risk intelligence score: relevance itself, diversity of experiences, and record keeping.

Sometimes we can increase the relevance of *old* experiences to a *new* problem. For example, suppose you must fix your roof. You have had better experience with one neighbor's repair recommendations than with others'. But the two of you have never talked about roofers. This is a case of striking but possibly irrelevant experience with a source of good advice. One remedy is to find out whether your neighbor's roof has misbehaved as much as the other parts of his house. You may find he has as much cause to know about roofers as about other kinds of contractors. See whether new aspects of old experiences rule out some possible (but wrong) solutions to the new problem.

But it often isn't possible to bootstrap the relevance of our experience. If you're facing a new political risk, for example, there may be no way to make your regularly scheduled meetings with customers, suppliers, and other providers relevant to it. You may have ten conversations scheduled in the next week with customers about the quality of the machine parts your company supplies. Yet there's just no way to bring, say, Turkey into every conversation, and even if you could, there's nothing most customers could tell you about it! It pays to be *creative* in developing experience, but not *quixotic.*

The second way to address a "relevance gap" in our personal or organizational experience is to widen that experience. If you're thinking of doing business in a new country, try a smaller contract to learn about how people do business there. In general, tackle a problem that seems to share root causes with the new risks you are evaluating.

For example, suppose your company is thinking of applying a firmwide planning system to a remote subsidiary for the first time. Is your implementation experience relevant to the subsidiary? If not, you may want to start with a smaller project that requires the subsidiary to integrate some of its processes with the rest of the company.

If your experience, however compelling, may be irrelevant to a new risk, find a way to diversify it. Remember that an experience's relevance depends on how many of the possible drivers of a new risk would make it certain or rule it out.

The third way to fight a tendency toward impressionism is consulting the record. You may not recall or know of experience in your organization relevant to a new risk, but it may be there. Reach out to your colleagues and ask. The biggest risk assessment failure most executives report is forgetting to ask other managers about their problem, however novel or unprecedented it seems to be.

The one thing *not* to do is back off from those memorable experiences. They have and should have enormous power in guiding our judgments where they apply. After all, highly improbable experiences that are directly relevant to a risk problem really *do* rule out a lot of possible causes of the risk. Anchoring on these kinds of experiences misleads us only where the experiences lack relevance. The trick is to be careful in applying them.

Encyclopedists

Encyclopedists have lots of experience that applies to the risks underlying new projects or risky decisions, but the experience teaches no strong lessons. The encyclopedist's experience applies to many risks but lacks impact because it suggests nothing about the risks that we would not have guessed. The second column in table 3-3 shows a typical pattern for the risk intelligence score of an encyclopedist.

The key gap in the encyclopedist's experience is surprise or *improbability.* For example, suppose you hired a very bright young assistant to help develop a new brand of fitness equipment. The assistant is well trained and has mastered an enormous amount of information on the fitness sector and marketing analytic techniques like survey research. If you want to know the population of greater Cleveland, you just ask him. He could win *Jeopardy* in a heartbeat. But his instincts don't seem well honed, because what he can tell you reflects little of the kind of surprising experience that focuses our beliefs.

Both military planners and businesses operating in sectors with lots of strategic uncertainty often find themselves in the position of the encyclopedist. No matter how many facts and figures they have mastered about opponents or competitors, the civilian population or customers, force requirements or costs, they don't have insight into how their challengers see the world and think. Or at least they haven't had a chance to battle-test their theories about how those challengers think.

The case of the encyclopedist is more general than that, however. In fact, it is a brand of inexperience. As academic and on-the-job training gets better and better, it's possible for people changing occupations or entering the workforce to learn huge amounts of facts that bear on the projects or decisions confronting an organization. But that training cannot replace the memorability of a few shocking experiences that give us our strongest sense of *how the world is not.* This is the predicament of the encyclopedist.

What can the encyclopedist do? The three principle remedies reflect elements of the risk intelligence score, but the remedies differ from the impressionist's: amount of experience, the memorability of that experience itself, and record keeping.

Raising the raw amount or frequency of one's experience related to a problem is rarely a practical solution for systematic weaknesses in risk assessment capabilities. This is because our jobs and personal lives generally force us to have as much contact with customers, neighbors, prospects, teachers, suppliers, friends, business service providers, home service providers, and providers of products related to ours as we can possibly have. But if our risk scores suggest we are encyclopedists, it means we are in some sense a little wet behind the ears in a variety of areas that matter. It means we haven't been shocked.

So if an encyclopedist you know is a great analyst with questionable instincts, see whether you can give that analyst a tour of duty in a customer-facing job. If you feel that your own experience is too cursory or bookish, then look for opportunities that maximize the time you spend out of your office or on the phone with people who have a point of view on the problem areas you are trying to manage. Minimize the synthetic work you do analyzing problems or writing memos, business cases, and marketing materials, and maximize the time you spend gleaning information that's harder to replicate.

The next remedy is to increase the memorability or content of the experiences you are already bound to have. Since surprise reflects the improbability of our experience, the remedy is to seek surprise. The best way to do that, if you have the opportunity, is to focus your time on people with unpredictable or even outright contrarian points of view. Find people who will provide the biggest challenge to how you think.

Conversations are not the only way to fix an experience gap, of course. Every event that defeats our expectations has a strong impact on our beliefs and sharpens our understanding because it rules out faulty suppositions about how things work. This means we can accelerate our learning by building conjectures into our home or office work flow. Ask every day what you expect will be the outcome of any transaction or event, no matter how small, that's relevant to the risk problem you're trying to solve. When things turn out differently, ask why.

Since those small surprises and explanations add up, record keeping looms large in improving the risk intelligence of the encyclopedist. But the reason is different from the importance of records to the impressionist. Here it's because it isn't always easy to identify common threads among past experiences that can bind together a clear and well-informed worldview in a new problem area.

For example, even if you pay careful attention to each surprising rejection you get in sales calls for a popular new investment product, it may be hard to see what really links them. There may be no substitute for keeping detailed notes, or even an electronic file that groups your "no thank you" prospects into segments. In this case, good records serve to build a series of small surprises into larger ones that narrow the possibilities of what may truly be driving sales.

Amnesiacs

The amnesiac has surprising, memorable experiences relevant to a broad variety of project choices, risky decisions, and problems challenging an organization. So what's not to love about the experience base of the amnesiac? The problem for people with this pattern of risk intelligence strengths and weaknesses is not just forgetting what they learn. It's failing to record it in a format others can use.

The amnesiac's risk intelligence pattern shows a gap under record keeping. But there is a corresponding strength under amount or frequency of experience. After all, record keeping gets more difficult as you have more to record. Table 3-3 shows what a typical risk intelligence pattern for an amnesiac looks like.

So amnesiacs have loads of raw experience. In fact, these "experience mines" are often useful to their organizations precisely because of their experience. But what they know cannot really accelerate the performance of a colleague unless it can reduce the colleague's personal dependence on them. In other words, amnesiacs must find ways to enrich their colleagues' experience with what they know or learn rather than just provide their colleagues with access to it.

This reflects the difference between the value of what Paul Romer calls wetware and software. Let's look at how he defines the two ideas.

> *Wetware captures what economists call human capital and what philosophers and cognitive scientists sometimes call tacit knowledge. It includes all the things stored in the "wet" computer of a person's human brain.*
>
> *Software includes all the knowledge that has been codified and can be transmitted to others: literal computer code, blueprints, mechanical drawings, operating instructions for machines, scientific principles, folk wisdom, films, books, musical recordings, the routines followed in a firm, the literal and figurative recipes we use, even the language we speak. It can be stored as text or drawings on paper, as images on film, or as a string of bits on a computer disk or a laser disk. Once the first copy of a piece of software has been produced, it can be reproduced, communicated and used simultaneously by an arbitrarily large number of people.*[6]

Karl Popper made a similar distinction between what we know and the actual records we make of what we know. He calls what we know, together with all our thoughts, the second world (as opposed to a first world of physical things). He distinguishes it from a third world of what we record so that others can use it. Popper thinks it is the latter that makes scientific advance possible.[7] But for Popper, the importance of a clear record is that it encourages objective criticism.

What can the amnesiac do about record keeping? More and better experience is not the answer. In this case, *none* of the risk intelligence elements contains a remedy. The only answer is systematically capturing the amnesiac's rich experience in a way that others can use. The issue is where organizations should place the burden for this.

Many organizations ask experience-rich employees to memorialize what they know, and punish them for lack of diligence in doing so. The problem with this is that none of us really "knows what we know." Asking us to get it all down on paper or spreadsheets assumes we can recognize something that feels instinctive to us.

It makes far more sense for companies to shift the burden in moving what amnesiacs know from wetware to software the rest of the firm can use. Rather than assume amnesiacs jealously guard their knowledge, organizations should ask other employees to debrief their amnesiacs through a formal interview process. The interviewers may even be in a better position than the amnesiacs they interview to recognize what matters and distill it.

Such a process need not seem dismissive, morbid, or funereal. It can instead be celebratory and reflect the recognition of a valuable stage in the life cycle of a manager.

THE THREE AGES OF RISK INTELLIGENCE

The encyclopedist, the impressionist, and the amnesiac represent three stages in a life cycle of risk assessment skills and the experience underlying them. Encyclopedists have lots of what may often resemble book knowledge, but lack memorable experiences that sharpen judgment. Impressionists have highly memorable knowledge but apply it indiscriminately in cases where it doesn't apply. Amnesiacs have rich stores of relevant, memorable experience but do not reliably record it for others to use. Together, they represent the youth, adulthood, and old age of risk intelligence.

And yet encyclopedists need not be young, and amnesiacs need not be old. We experience many cycles of learning throughout our lives, and we are likely to veer into these three risk intelligence traps at many times. The trick is to recognize them.

From the perspective of the organization, however, there is one further possibility. That is grouping encyclopedists, impressionists, and amnesiacs to complement one another. A task force with an encyclopedist will have rich background knowledge. A task force with an impressionist will be decisive. A task force with an amnesiac will avoid errors. Together, the three can be formidable.

Organizations may want to consider inventorying the risk intelligence skill portfolios of critical operating units. These risk intelligence inventories can help ensure that groups struggling with new risks broadly cover the capabilities needed to make good judgments about them. The threefold goal should be to break up clusters of encyclopedists, impressionists, and amnesiacs; make sure critical risk-facing groups have at least one of each; and try to up everyone's game.

Above all, the three ages of risk intelligence can overcome their weaknesses by working closely together. "Enhancing Risk Intelligence Through Teams" explains how you can actually balance a team's risk intelligence.

HOW RISK INTELLIGENCE SCORES VALUE INFORMATION

At the heart of the risk intelligence score is an effort to put a value on experience or, more generally, information. This section makes a case for the score's potential robustness as such a measure of value. The final section in this chapter proposes a quantitative definition of relevance that is compatible with a formal definition of information content (corresponding to the element of surprise in the risk intelligence score). Readers can pass over these somewhat more technical sections and move straight on to the strategic implications of risk intelligence in chapter 4 without losing the thread of the argument.

There's nothing arbitrary about the elements of the risk intelligence score. For example, the elements for the amount of experience and diversity of experience reflect the fact that more, and more varied, experience will always accelerate learning. Without record keeping, others can't benefit from that learning.

Enhancing Risk Intelligence Through Teams

It makes intuitive sense that teams balancing the characteristics of encyclopedists, impressionists, and amnesiacs could develop strong risk intelligence in a wide variety of areas. But execution looks hard. How can you tell whether a colleague is more like an encyclopedist, an impressionist, or an amnesiac?

A sign of a budding encyclopedist is indecisiveness or a recurring need of guidance. Remember that encyclopedists lack the memorable or surprising experiences that often help us make up our minds. But why would one employee miss surprising experiences more than another?

Most of us are exposed to similar experiences in the workplace. But some may seek out surprises, while others seek comfort in what's familiar. Those who seek comfort in the familiar may deprive themselves of the bracing experiences that build decisiveness.

A related sign of an emerging encyclopedist is the tendency to follow peers. It may be that he fears making mistakes. If he avoids mistakes, he'll avoid surprises. But if he avoids surprises, he won't develop strong impressions. If that means less decisiveness, it becomes easier to follow the crowd.

The classic remedy for an employee who follows the crowd too much is to embrace mistakes. Ask him to go out and make some— preferably small ones. They'll provide confidence as well as good stories to tell.

A sign that a colleague or an employee is developing into an impressionist would be too much independence, to the point of willfulness. We usually interpret inflexibility as stubbornness. But it could also reflect an effort to apply a few memorable lessons learned about the job too indiscriminately. It could come across as bossiness.

(continued)

If impressionism, in the sense of this chapter, is the diagnosis, what is the cause? Determining exactly what memorable experiences have made the strongest impression on a colleague can be very hard. But it may be worth trying to reconstruct the surprising or memorable experiences that have caused an employee to become judgmental, inflexible, or uncompromising. If you can do so, it will be easier to make out where those strong lessons learned just don't apply.

Finally, you might think a colleague must suffer memory loss to be an amnesiac. But this section takes *amnesiac* in a different sense. Here, an emerging amnesiac would be someone who, however rich in experience, shares little of it. This may have nothing to do with selfishness. The risk intelligence amnesiac may simply not see the point of reformulating what she's learned.

This type of behavior can also lead to introversion and, when it does, should be distinguished from the forced introversion of the impressionist. The impressionist risks being bossy; the amnesiac, too guarded.

Group tasks where many heads perform better than one may get the amnesiac to be more forthcoming. In fact, this leads back to the overall prescription of putting together teams with complementary risk intelligence strengths and weaknesses.

But the roots of the two central elements of relevance and surprise lie deeper. Their role in the score is to measure the relative value of an organization's typical single experience for assessing a risk. The other elements then extrapolate that measure to the overall experience and record keeping of the organization with respect to the risk.

So the measures for relevance and surprise must gauge the usefulness of a typical observation or piece of evidence for solving a risk problem. If the solution is one of a set of alternative hypotheses about the risk, relevance and surprise must measure the usefulness of any piece of evidence for choosing among the alternatives.

This is exactly like the problem of calculating how a piece of evidence affects the probability of alternative hypotheses. Fortunately, the dissident English cleric Thomas Bayes solved that problem in a paper published posthumously in 1764.[8]

Bayes found a way to relate the probability of competing hypotheses, given some new evidence, to the probability of the hypotheses without the evidence. For example, suppose you run a neighborhood newspaper and are thinking about buying a local Internet news site called "makeitupyourself.com." If its advertising plans were accurate, you would be willing to pay $100,000 for it. Without knowing anything more than you do now, you would pay $5,000. It's as if you thought the advertising plans had a 5 percent probability of being right.

But the editor tells you about a market research focus group that can test the advertising plans. What Bayes found lets you calculate what you should pay, given your $5,000 starting point and certain characteristics of the focus group. Here are some examples. Bayes's formula says you should pay the following:

- $25,000, given a successful test from a panel that approves 20 percent of all the plans it reviews and 100 percent of the ones that later prove accurate

- $25,000, given a successful test from a panel that approves 10 percent of all the plans it reviews and 50 percent of the ones that later prove accurate

- $50,000, given a successful test from a panel that approves 10 percent of all the plans it reviews and 100 percent of the ones that later prove accurate

Two factors are at work here. The third panel tells more than the first one because its successful tests are more surprising (10 percent versus

20 percent). Its results are more memorable. The third panel tells more than the second one because its tests are more discriminating (no false negatives versus 50 percent for the second panel). Its results are more relevant. If other bidders for makeitupyourself.com are putting together test panels, you want the one with the most surprise and relevance. That's just what the core elements of the risk intelligence score estimate.

For those who prefer math, here's what Bayes's formula and its expressions for surprise and relevance look like. If h is a hypothesis like "the plans are right," e is the evidence from a test, and P means "probability of," Bayes's theorem looks like this:

$$P(h \text{ given } e) = P(h) * [\text{FACTORS}]$$

The *factors* are the probability of the evidence if the hypothesis is true and the probability of the evidence no matter what hypothesis is true. The whole expression is:

$$P(h \text{ given } e) = P(h) * [P(e \text{ given } h) / P(e)]$$

It may help to relate the formula term by term back to the bid suggested by a successful test from the third focus research panel. The $50,000 bid recommendation means there's a 50 percent chance that the advertising plans are right, given a successful test. It equals the 5 percent initial probability times a 100 percent probability of a successful test, given an accurate plan, divided by a 10 percent probability of a successful test for all plans.

The idea behind the factors is that an improbable observation or experience [corresponding to a low $P(e)$] might tell you a lot about what is not true of the world. For example, a successful result from a panel that approves just 10 percent of all plans tells you that whatever makes it disapprove 90 percent of them isn't true of yours. This is why the risk intelligence score gives improbable experiences high marks for surprise.

Even improbable experiences may be irrelevant if they're consistent with most of the alternative hypotheses or expectations about the risk problem, however. This would be true of an observation that, however surprising, is still possible under every alternative theory of the risk. Relevant experiences let you reject alternative hypotheses or expectations because they're inconsistent with them [corresponding to $P(e$ given $h) = 0$].

But there's more to relevance. Your confidence in the surviving hypotheses or solutions to a risk problem goes up if an observation lets you kick out a lot of inconsistent ones. But you feel even better if some of the survivors would make the observation 100 percent probable [corresponding to $P(e$ given $h) = 100$ percent]. For example, the panel that approves 100 percent of all plans that turn out to be accurate is useful because it produces no false negatives. A bad result is decisive. So the risk intelligence score gives the highest relevance marks to evidence made certain by some alternatives and impossible by others.

Since plenty of interesting hypotheses have a probability of zero—especially if they relate to an infinite number of possible observations—you should take the relation with a grain of salt.[9] But the factors for surprise and relevance relating the "before" and "after" probabilities of a hypothesis provide a concrete framework for thinking about learning.

RELEVANCE AS THE MISSING LINK BETWEEN INFORMATION AND LEARNING

Suppose you meet a really happy customer who says your planning system is the best thing that ever happened to his business. But the only reason he can give is that it was right for him. The meeting felt great—but proved irrelevant to what will drive sales.

On the way back to the office, you pick up a dirty matchbook. In it is printed the slogan "Think what your customer will need tomorrow."

The idea of designing what your customers will have wanted rather than what they think they need now gets you over a crucial design hurdle. A mundane experience proves immediately relevant.

Measuring relevance separately from surprise could solve a lot of practical problems in managing information as well as business risks. Up to now, those trying to estimate the value of a piece of information have tended to ignore relevance since it is hard to measure. Without such a measure, we mostly avoid trying to price information.

Setting relevance aside goes back to the first practical definition of information. In 1948, a Bell Labs engineer named Claude Shannon tackled the problem of measuring the information content of a message. His colleagues may have hoped it would at least distract him from riding his frightening unicycles around the corridors of the building after hours.[10] He ultimately triumphed, showing how to measure not just information but also the capacity of a channel to transmit it without errors. But his work on content eclipsed the question of how relevant information was to any particular problem.

He wrote that, as a first approximation, the amount of information conveyed by one character of a message was the number of alternative characters that might have appeared at that point in the message.[11] So for a twenty-six-letter alphabet, the information conveyed by each actual letter of a message would be a function of twenty-six.

He refined the idea to what a later writer called the "surprisal" of the character, meaning its improbability.[12] A character's surprisal varies with the inverse of its probability. But the inverse of the probability of a piece of information is exactly the factor for its surprise or memorability. So Shannon's measure of information resembles the parts of Bayes's formula and the risk intelligence score that assess the improbability or surprise of a piece of evidence.

But information can be surprising without being relevant. Specifically, an observation, experience, or piece of evidence does you little good if it's equally likely under every alternative hypothesis or solution for the problem you're trying to solve. Suppose, for example, the probability of the evidence is one-eighth. Shannon would say it contains 3 bits (digits that can be 0 or 1) of information. But that evidence can't help you choose an alternative if it has exactly the same 3-bit probability given the truth of every hypothesis or solution you're considering.

We should be able to measure the relevance of the evidence to our efforts to solve the problem. In the preceding example, a good measure of relevance would be –3. That would precisely offset Shannon's measure of the evidence's information content.

The crucial difference between relevance and the concepts of surprise, improbability, and information content is that the latter are independent of your problem. A rare and surprising observation is rare and surprising regardless of whether you can put it to use. But relevance depends on the problem you want to solve. More specifically, it depends on the hypotheses, solutions, or conjectures you have proposed to solve your problem.

For example, suppose blue smoke starts to billow from under the hood of your car anytime you drive over 60 mph. You also notice, for the first time, a mysterious green liquid collect under your car when it's parked. So you call the guys at *Car Talk*.

They tell you the green liquid is irrelevant. They think the smoke comes from a combustion problem, friction in the belts, or an oil leak. In other words, they have three alternative theories for the problem. The green liquid could appear in a scenario corresponding to any one of their alternative theories.

But suppose you have a fourth theory. You noticed a similar green liquid at the car wash and noticed that the fuel cap came off just before your car went through it. Your theory is that the gas in the tank got contaminated.

Now they agree that the green liquid is relevant. It's relevant not to the problem of billowing blue smoke in general. Rather, it's relevant to your hypothesis or conjecture about the cause of the problem and its solution.

Here is a formula for the relevance of a piece of evidence, e, to a set of hypotheses, h_i, for solving a problem. In the expression, $P(h_i)$ and $P(e)$ are the probabilities of hypothesis i and evidence e, and $P(e/h_i)$ is the probability of e if h_i is true.

Relevance of e to the $h_i = \Sigma_i P(h_i/e) * \log_2 P(e/h_i)$

The formula captures the extent to which e discriminates among the h_i. It averages terms that are most negative where e is inconclusive about one of the h_i, and least negative or zero where one of the h_i would make e certain or impossible. The weights ensure that the whole thing is the negative of e's information content in cases where it's completely irrelevant. The formula uses base 2 logs to be consistent with Shannon's measure.

This means that with enough data, you could add the measure for the surprise or content of your typical experience [technically $-\log P(e)$] and its relevance to any set of risk hypotheses you're evaluating [$\Sigma_i P(h_i/e) * \log_2 P(e/h_i)$]. The result would measure the contribution of that experience to your risk intelligence for the risk.

Modern information theory has generally overtaken the fields that try to apply it. That's true here, too. Information theory has defined concepts satisfied by the surprise, as defined in Shannon, and the relevance, as defined here, of a set of observations.

The expected value across all possible related experiences of their content or surprise is called the *entropy* of that set of experiences. Higher entropy means typical experiences are more surprising.

The expected value across all possible related experiences of their relevance to a set of hypotheses is called the *conditional entropy* of the experiences given the hypotheses. Lower conditional entropy (less negative as defined here) indicates greater relevance.

Intriguingly, the sum of the two (or the difference as defined in textbooks) is the *mutual information* between the experiences and the hypotheses. It reflects how much one tells about the other.[13] The risk intelligence score tries to reduce all of this to a practical and intuitive tool.

4

Conducting a Risk
Strategy Audit

Look at some of the lists you have made recently. Some will be shopping lists or errands to do. But many, if not most, of the others probably imply choices about risk. A project list, for example, implies exposure to the risks reflecting what's uncertain about the costs and benefits of the items on it. These could be projects for your team at the office, personal work goals, tasks around the house, or even projects for your kids. Whatever kinds of projects are on your list, though, they fix a set of risks you will face as you work through them. To the extent you have chosen to pursue the projects, you have chosen their principal risks. They make up your *risk strategy*.

Of course, projects are not the only items that are risky. Lists of decisions imply a risk strategy just as much as lists of projects. So do lists of investments and initiatives. Lists of courses, trips, process improvement opportunities, lines of business, major purchases, athletic matches, and even dates all imply a risk strategy. What these lists have in common is *implied choice*. That choice shapes not just payoffs but also risks. How the risks fit together is the risk strategy we have chosen, intentionally or not.

Once you are armed with a way to score your risk intelligence or learning speed for the main risks you face, you can begin to see where your risk strategy is taking you. You need a way to monitor how well you are managing all of your big risks together. Since external and internal organizational dynamics change your risk exposure all the time, moreover, you may need to reevaluate your risks on a regular basis. The tool most of us pull off the shelf to do this is the *portfolio.* But it's not the right tool.

Brokers, investment advisers, and even Social Security reformers talk constantly about securities portfolios and sometimes even about risk portfolios. And why shouldn't they? Since the risks of different securities diversify one another, portfolios generally have lower risk, in the sense of volatility or value at risk, than their parts. In a sense, the risk of a securities portfolio is *more* important than the risk of its constituent securities.

But security risks are random, not learnable. So no notion of risk assessment expertise or risk intelligence enters into the picture. The only issue is how well the risks in a portfolio diversify one another. Portfolios are good tools for thinking about that.

The trouble is that we use portfolios to think about problems where risk diversification is not the only issue. For example, corporate strategists talk about a company's portfolio of businesses. Finance executives talk about their firm's portfolio of business risks. My father talks about the portfolio of carpentry projects that wait for him in the garage. A neighbor even talks about her kids' portfolio of after-school activities!

That's pretty heavy usage for a tool that's really designed for a different kind of risk. This chapter argues that portfolios are an inadequate tool for managing learnable risks. We must also think of our risks as presenting a *pipeline* of learning challenges, and then manage that pipeline. This leads to the third rule of risk intelligence:

Rule 1. Recognize which risks are learnable.

Rule 2. Identify risks you can learn about fastest.

Rule 3. Sequence risky projects in a "learning pipeline."

MASTERING ONE RISK AT A TIME

The risk intelligence score helps us measure our natural assessment capabilities for any particular risk. It's good to know what we're good at knowing. But those capabilities aren't cast in stone. There are times when we must pursue a project or make a decision regardless of how ill equipped we are to learn what drives its particular risks. At times like these, we must improve our capabilities. We must speed up how fast we can learn about the new risks we must embrace.

This imperative to push personal or organizational learning in new directions can put a limit on how many new projects or problems we should undertake. Many departments and divisions of companies take on risky projects one at a time; they learn about the risks underlying each project before moving to the next set of risks. They take a step-by-step approach and build a *pipeline* of risks.

Suppose, for example, that the staff members of Eat Press decide to launch a new imprint focusing on memoirs. They will invest large amounts of energy and money to start their new list of books. When the imprint launches, the firm will focus tremendous excitement and energy on the venture. This is fortunate because doing business in new publishing categories often poses unfamiliar risks that publishers must learn to manage.

The problem is that companies (and for that matter, people) aren't very good at learning very different things at the same time. When publishers try to build multiple lists in different markets that have very different characteristics, for example, they almost invariably run into serious operating challenges and often suffer unnecessary setbacks. But we often must place bets where we don't enjoy advantages. So we must devote time and resources to developing those advantages. In our hypothetical case, Eat Press must sequence the learning challenges in its risk pipeline by taking on projects that raise unfamiliar risks one at a time.

Let's say Eat Press moves forward with publishing memoirs, but as a cookbook specialist, it recognizes that it has no experience in the category. It might make sense to start with books by celebrity chefs. The food connection gives the publisher a learning advantage—or at least minimizes Eat's disadvantages relative to other publishers.

Over time, the staff will develop contacts and a greatly refined market sense for the memoir category the company once barely knew. If Eat scored its intelligence for risks in the memoir market, it would find it had improved in some or all of the score's elements.

It might, for example, find that its contacts with memoir buyers for bookstore chains were more *frequent*. The editors might find their professional conversations more *relevant* to what drives the memoir market as those conversations generate anecdotes supporting (or refuting) alternate explanations for success.

Eat's marketers might report more *surprising and telling* experiences in securing shelf space for perhaps unlikely memoir titles. Acquisition editors might report contacts with authors providing a usefully *different* perspective on the memoir market. And Eat might find itself starting to *formalize* what it was learning about the new market through biweekly cross-department meetings on its developing memoir list.

The story of a food imprint's foray into memoirs illustrates something we all experience. From time to time, we invest time and resources not just to *learn* about a new set of uncertainties but to *expand* our ability to learn about them. This can fundamentally change a risk intelligence score. But it's not easy, and the resource and organizational commitment it requires means focusing on one new risk at a time. The resource drag may even determine how often we can undertake fundamentally new initiatives.

SUCCESS, EXPOSURE GROWTH, AND
THE LAW OF RISK GRAVITY

To understand this "speed limit" on new initiatives, consider what happens if we succeed. What happens *after* we transform the frequency, relevance, surprise, diversity, and record keeping of our experiences relating to a new risk?

Go back to the food imprint. If Eat Press's bet pays off, its memoir list would occupy more resources in the organization. And that means the risks inherent in the memoir market would loom larger in its operational results. A bad memoir season, for example, might now affect a significant portion of the firm's total revenue.

Consequently, the people working on memoirs for Eat Press will experience some of the growing pains of any new line of business. The freedom they enjoy as a tiny in-house venture will give way to more and more oversight from top management. But this is not just because of the growing resources that the venture consumes.

The scrutiny that growing projects or lines of business attract increases because their risks affect more of the total performance of the organization. While new initiatives stay small, they generally help diversify the organization's overall risks. As they grow, they start to drive the organization's overall risks. Call it a law of gravity for risk.

Should it really be the risk and not the revenue or profit contribution of a firm's lines of business that commands top management attention? For example, should a company pay more attention to its largest business, like cookbooks in the publishing example, or to its most volatile line, like the memoir initiative? The answer is that companies should worry about where surprises are most likely to arise. So if our imaginary publisher is more likely to be wrong about the results of its little memoir line than its cookbooks, management should focus on memoirs.

Growth of a new business initiative also has an important impact on the diversity of a firm's other risks. As its new business grows, the firm must be careful about how the risks of further ventures relate to the risks of the successful one. For example, new categories like kiss-and-tell books or political insider tales might once have held out the promise of smoothing Eat's business results. But that's less likely if similar forces link those categories and memoirs. As Eat's memoir list grows, the things that will diversify its risks as a business must change.

Success is beginning to look like a pain in the neck for the memoir team. First they must endure greater scrutiny from top management. Then they get a lot of calls from the business development group checking out how closely they think various possible new Eat Press imprints may resemble memoirs. But one more shoe is about to drop. That's competition.

WHY DISCONTINUOUS ATTACKS DON'T ALWAYS REQUIRE DISCONTINUOUS TECHNOLOGIES

Traditionally, business managers and investors have acted as if risk affects most competitors in a given product or service market equally—or in proportion to the competitors' exposure to it. It's probably becoming clear that I think this is wrong. Previous chapters showed how differences in assessment skills can divide the players in any risk area into winners and losers. But the diversity of challengers' other risks can also help them take on a risky market's leader.

This may seem like a contradiction. If great risk intelligence distinguishes leaders, then why should a challenger distracted by diverse risks have a shot?

Consider, first of all, that success attracts attention. Suppose other cookbook publishers see the memoir coup of Eat Press and begin publishing their own famous-chef memoirs. Suddenly, the competitors are learning and benefiting from Eat's experience. Competitors keep their learning costs down by riding on the leader's coattails.

Consider next that followers sometimes develop a risk intelligence advantage over leaders who understand their risks well. Clayton Christensen explained in *The Innovator's Dilemma* that successful firms often face disruptive competition from what *look* like marginal competitors using what *looks* like inferior technology.[1] In fact, those marginal competitors may be learning a new way to compete by trying to meet the needs of a set of underserved customers.

But even though it's the underserved customers who are the key to these "attacks from below," the threat to entrenched firms comes in the form of successful—and often cheaper—new technologies. Christensen calls the innovations based on these new technologies "discontinuous" because they represent a break from the prevailing technological orthodoxy in the market.

A discontinuous innovation in the Eat Press illustration might be audiocassettes of scripted but unpublished great-chef memoirs. Perhaps there's a niche market of people preparing dinner at night who can't chop and read at the same time.

Christensen's story might make it appear that the only way such disruptive attacks can succeed is if there is *some* new technology to be found in your area of business. But the more you think about how risk affects competition, the more pervasive these threats that Christensen identified start to appear. There is at least one more way that risk can help challengers attack a leader who seems to understand it well.

It's easiest to explain this final way that risk affects competition by example. So consider that our food publisher must pay more attention to the quirks—the risks—of the memoir market as its memoir list grows. But that's not entirely true for publishers outside of the category.

Sure, challengers must learn about the new market's risks. Since they will be starting small, however, the risks of their major business activities will probably diversify or cushion their exposure to the risks of the memoir market. That means the new risks of the memoir market won't contribute much to the overall risk of a competing publisher. And that means they won't raise its cost of capital.

On the other hand, risks in the memoir market are contributing a larger and larger part of the overall risks of Eat Press and increasing the costs of *its* capital. In other words, Eat Press will have to pay more for every extra dollar it raises to expand its memoir list than new competitors will initially have to pay to finance their own lists.

This is true even if everything else about Eat and its new memoir competitors that might affect their financing cost is the same. Of course, the extra financing cost that Eat faces may be small beer compared to the learning costs that its challengers face. But in the long run, it makes a huge difference that it's cheaper to finance a small, diversified attack on a risky market than defend a concentrated position in it.[2]

This last way that risk intelligence can intensify competition gives new meaning to *discontinuous attacks*. Christensen focuses on how challengers can take on experienced players with *discontinuous innovations* based on new or repurposed technologies. This last effect is far more general. It doesn't rely on discontinuous innovation. It relies only on discontinuous opportunities. It arises anytime an opportunity is discontinuous from the rest of a challenger's business activities so that its old risks can cushion the firm's exposure to new ones.

Of course, those newcomers must still determine how to contain the cost of learning about the risks associated with whatever business activity they're entering. But their investors probably won't punish them for the risk until it's too big to diversify. This is one reason why Eat Press will never want to rest on its laurels in the memoir market: it must keep improving its ability to learn about the market because the only thing that will protect it in the long run is its advantage in assessing the market's evolving risks.

In sum, there are three ways risk affects competition. First, competitors can learn from a leader's experience. Second, as Christensen explained, competitors can learn from the needs of fringe customers the leader has not had time to learn how to serve.

But the third reason has been largely overlooked. Other players will dabble in our growth businesses simply because most of their risks are very different. They may not understand the new risks they are shouldering as well as we do. But if those new risks are uncorrelated with their current business, they may be able to offset them better. Our only defense is to make sure we can keep learning about them more easily and cheaply. Leaders have a simple choice: occupy a niche no one wants to challenge, or *lead*.

THE PIPELINE IN THE PORTFOLIO

The last three sections traced the life cycle of a project or initiative and the risks underlying it through three stages. In "Mastering One Risk at a Time," we selected projects based on what risks we thought we could learn, and invested in the learning skills they required. In "Success, Exposure Growth, and the Law of Risk Gravity," some of those projects or initiatives grew to have an impact on not only our organization's revenue and profit but also its overall risk. In "Why Discontinuous Attacks Don't Always Require Discontinuous Technologies," unrelated businesses found they could finance diversified experiments in the area of our projects more cheaply than we could finance their expansion. But these challengers faced offsetting costs in learning about their new risks.

When challengers enter our market and start to compete for our customers, we cannot stand still. We must keep learning about the market's risks. But from time to time, we must let go of a line of business even if we have dominated it. We'll usually let go when challengers can learn about its risks as easily as we do. So we must develop new projects in case the old ones falter. And this takes us back to the beginning of the life cycle of our projects and the risks behind them.

What this means is that we can't wait too long to explore risky new opportunities. The lesson of "Mastering One Risk at a Time" is that no group or team should take on too many challenges requiring the mastery of new risks at the same time. But we can't hold off tackling new risks until challengers overtake our lead in old ones. So we must build pipelines that space out the new project and decision risks we will need to learn and master.

Risk pipelines are like new-product pipelines. Risks follow a life cycle, running through our stages of dabbling in them, mastering the learning challenges they pose, harvesting them, and exiting them. We must select initiatives and projects so that our risk pipeline matches this natural risk life cycle. If we do not, we will either overwhelm ourselves with new learning challenges or face learning crises where we start losing our bets to those who find ways to analyze our risks more effectively.

Pipelines are not portfolios. We build portfolios of risks to benefit from how they offset one another, from their diversity. But the life cycle of learnable risks pushes us to sequence them in pipelines like new products. Must we choose?

We can do both. We can determine the life cycle stage of each learnable risk in any portfolio of risks. This will let us see the portfolio in terms of which risks we are learning about, which ones are coming to dominate our overall business, and which ones we may need to harvest. This will let us see the pipeline in the portfolio.

Pipelines apply to individuals' as well as companies' risks. How we approach personal risks may put pipelines and portfolios in perspective. After all, everyone can remember learning different lessons at different times.

Think of the difference between a Rhodes scholar who plays sports and a star college athlete hoping to make the pros. Many athletes put their time and effort against a single risk—their sport. If they don't make it to the professional ranks, they will have fewer career alternatives after all the time they've devoted to it. The Rhodes scholar, on the other hand, hedges her strategy. She pursues sports at a competitive level and competes successfully in other areas as well. The main difference between the two may seem to be that the Rhodes scholar builds a portfolio of academic and athletic efforts.

But she isn't trying to create near-term options so she can pursue a second one if the first one doesn't pan out. In a true portfolio strategy, the Rhodes scholar would stay as flexible as possible to see which pursuit offered the greatest promise. Instead, she is laying the groundwork to learn different lessons at different times.

The Rhodes scholar is managing risks across their—and her—life cycle so that as she gets older, she can take on different challenges and new risks. She cultivates athletic skills while it's still easy to get out on a field and run but develops learning habits to help her succeed in other endeavors later in life. It's a pipeline strategy after all.

Pipelines shed a new light on the decisions we make regarding risk, but they don't preclude the traditional notion of portfolios. Even a pure pipeline strategy builds up a changing portfolio of risks over time. But there is a tension here, and it is between the strength of the assessment skills we bring to a risk and the extent to which our other risks offset it. Risk intelligence and diversification can and do conflict, and we must understand how.

TRADING OFF DIVERSIFICATION AND RISK INTELLIGENCE

There's always a trade-off in our risk strategies. On the one hand, project risks that are diverse will tend to offset one another and reduce our exposure to any one risk. So all things being equal, we ought to prefer a list of projects with diverse risks. If all our projects depend on clear skies, for example, a spell of bad weather can shut us down. But if some require warm days and some require cool days, we can make progress under almost any conditions.

Our assessment skills for those project risks, on the other hand, will vary. And the more diverse the risks are, the less consistently effective we'll be in assessing them. All things being equal, we'd prefer a project list concentrating on risks we can assess well. So diversity can be a drawback. For example, I knew a consultant with a real gift for assessing boardroom politics. He took a position in industry but never felt good about it. He eventually went back to consulting, concluding that boardroom uncertainties vary less across firms than general management risks do within them.

Of course, it would be great to find a diversified risk strategy where we enjoyed consistently strong risk intelligence. But that might be a rarity. We'd better hope to the contrary that we never get tasked with a strategy concentrated on risks we're terrible at assessing. But what about the other combinations of diversification and risk intelligence we might encounter in a risk strategy? How much diversification should we give up to focus a risk strategy on our risk intelligence strengths? How much risk intelligence should we sacrifice for better diversification?

This is like a classic problem for bank commercial credit and loan managers. Banks can focus on commercial sectors they understand really well, such as print shops. Call them "high risk intelligence" strategies. On the other hand, banks can seek diversification in their loan portfolios so they can weather downturns in specific sectors. These would be "high diversification" strategies. Well-run banks seek a mixture of sector expertise and diversification in their commercial loans.

Here, what has always applied to banks is beginning to affect the rest of us. Of course, we have always faced a trade-off between the challenges that cater to our strengths and the ones that offset other risks. But we have never had so many information tools to track our results and reveal how those risks really play out. It's one of those situations where now that we *can* worry about it, we *must* worry about it.

So we need a tool to put our risk intelligence and diversification into perspective. Let's look at a way of picturing how they come together in a risk strategy.

THE RISK STRATEGY MATRIX

How can you picture a risk strategy? This is the part of the book where I roll out a two-by-two matrix, and you wonder why business writers are so addicted to these pictures. After all, there must be other ways to illustrate how two items vary.

But there are two other reasons why I want to use a two-by-two matrix to picture risk strategies. First, there's an important analogy between this approach and the granddaddy of all two-by-two matrices—Boston Consulting Group's (BCG's) *growth-share matrix* for picturing growth strategies. Second, risks flow through this matrix in a characteristic way. The matrix helps keep track of the flow.

The matrix is just dots of different sizes on a two-by-two grid. The dots stand for the major risks of a risk strategy. Those risks could correspond to projects, problems, lines of business, initiatives, decisions, responsibilities, after-school activities, hobbies, romantic interests—whatever set of challenges raise uncertainties. It's easiest to think of each dot as standing for the principal risk of a project, division, or task.

The size of each dot can reflect one of two things. Ideally, it would reflect the size of the risk, measured to a common standard. That standard might be value at risk for a given level of confidence. Often, however, it's good enough to approximate exposure to project risks with some measure of the size of the projects. Such a measure might be current or expected revenue. Another measure, more appropriate for projects on the home front, might be expected time consumed.

The position of the dots depends, naturally, on two things. The vertical position measures how poorly each risk correlates with the others on the grid; the horizontal measures how well we can assess it. The higher the dot, the more the other risks offset it. The farther right the dot, the better our risk intelligence for that risk.

This means that each risk strategy matrix (see figure 4-1) is specific for a person or an organization. And it's also specific to the risks of something like a list of projects.

Let me emphasize how the matrix shows the life cycle of a risk. We constantly scour the landscape for projects whose risks place them in the upper-left corner, where we don't have any particular learning advantages—yet. But we have the potential to raise our learning speed for assessing some of them to best in class. For example, we may decide to investigate direct marketing for some of our company's products.

When we think we can build a learning or information advantage in one of those risks, we invest in that ability. We may hope to learn more about it or build a better risk management data set for it. In the direct marketing example, we might hire someone with expertise or develop real knowledge of it ourselves. Consequently, the project moves to the upper right of the grid, reflecting higher comparative risk assessment skills.

If the project succeeds, its principal risk grows in relation to the whole project list. The risk can then no longer diversify the overall

FIGURE 4-1

Risk strategy matrix

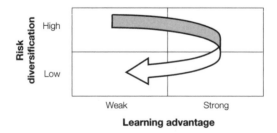

risk strategy as much as it could when it was a smaller part of it. For example, direct marketing might become a center of excellence for the whole company. Problems such as new direct marketing regulations could then have a material impact on firmwide results. To reflect this, the risk drops to the lower right of the grid as if under the force of gravity.

Now we've reached the point where newcomers may be in a better position to compete with us. After all, they won't have as much exposure to the project's risk as we have. So their other risks may better offset it. This is a good time for us to build new skills in case the venture becomes unattractive. For example, we may divert resources to account management that are currently devoted to direct marketing. On the grid, the risk slips to the left as others improve their comparative ability to learn about it and assess it.

In the direct marketing example, risks underlying a new sales approach went through a migration. We got better at learning about them, they grew in relation to other business risks, and we eventually deemphasized them. The two-by-two grid shows this as a clockwise flow, as if a pipeline wound around the grid from upper left to lower left.

The story of Lehman Brothers provides a concrete example. Known for decades as an equity house, the firm helped bring the airline industry public. But by the time it stumbled with some new hybrid equity products in the 1980s, it had too much exposure to the equity markets (shown in figure 4-2 in the lower-right cell). Its mergers and acquisitions business (upper right) was still going strong, but the ebbs and flows of deal making were starting to dominate the swings in the company's bottom line. So the firm started to build out its fixed income, or bond, business (upper left in figure 4-2). It was a good move—bonds would become the profit driver through the next decade.

Pfizer provides a contrasting example. For years, investors have pressured the company to extend its pipeline of potential blockbuster drugs—and hence its pipeline of risks in testing and marketing new

FIGURE 4-2

Risk strategy matrix for Lehman (circa 1990)

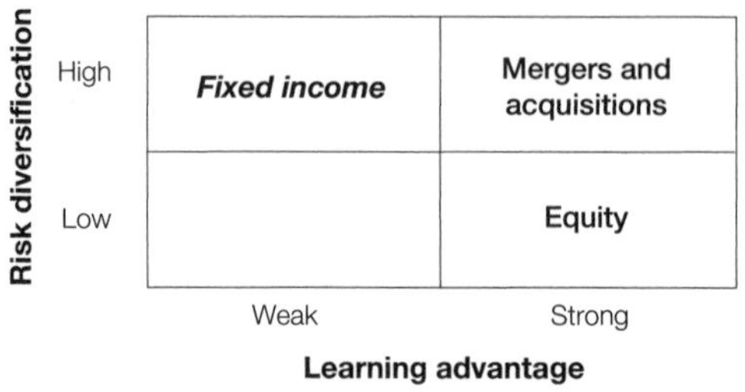

types of drugs. The fear is that the firm may not find another Lipitor, the popular drug that cuts bad cholesterol. So Pfizer built an extremely diversified drug pipeline.

A lot of those drugs have had troubles in clinical trials, though. Some argue that's to be expected, since Pfizer is competing in many areas of pharmacology involving different biological and even regulatory challenges. But it may have become too diversified, and it's changing tack. The firm is developing a drug called "torcetrapib" that may complement Lipitor. It raises good cholesterol just as Lipitor lowers the bad. They might make a profitable pair. More importantly for this discussion, Pfizer's vast experience in the market for drugs managing cholesterol help serve it well with torcetrapib. Torcetrapib fills a hole in the pipeline between Pfizer's diversifed projects and Lipitor (see upper-right cell in figure 4-3).

The difference between Lehman and Pfizer is that Lehman was riding on the crest of a wave and needed another wave. The grid reflects this with the two older risks clustered to the right. Pfizer was in danger of seeing Lipitor, one of its best products, lose share to competitors without a replacement. It needed to move something down the pipeline quickly. The hole in Pfizer's pipeline that the grid shows before adding torcetrapib would have become more pronounced had Lipitor slipped to the lower left.

The situations and responses of the two companies differed. But they sought something similar in their risk strategies. They sought a balance between risk diversification and the expertise they brought to those risks.

RISK STRATEGY AUDITS

A risk strategy audit is a step-by-step review of how your own individual risks or the principal risks in your organization fit together. It asks questions to determine the diversification within your risk strategy of each of your risks. And it asks you to rate your risk intelligence for each of them.

Risk strategy audits can be very simple and very complex. Complex ones would involve statistical estimates of risk correlations and survey assessments of risk intelligence from operating managers. Simple ones sketched in an armchair with paper and pencil and a little careful reflection can also be amazingly revealing.

The usefulness of risk strategy audits does not depend on objectivity. In fact, objectivity is out of the question for simple risk strategy audits. While it's possible to determine objective values for the diversification of each risk, risk intelligence scores are inherently subjective. And even if you could make them more objective, there is

FIGURE 4-3

Risk strategy matrix for Pfizer (circa 2004)

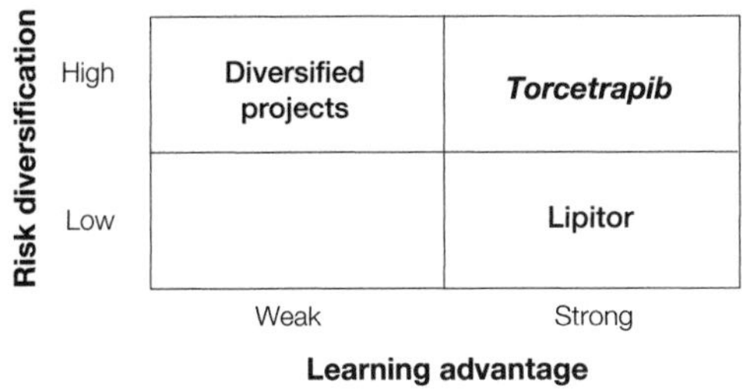

little need to do so. What matters is how you rate your risk intelligence for each risk *compared* with your risk intelligence for the others. If you're a tough grader, everything shifts to the left on your risk strategy matrix. If you're easy, it all shifts to the right.

Figure 4-4 is a simple example of a risk strategy audit.

Risk intelligence

For each project, answer the five questions with a 0 for "less than competitors," a 1 for "the same as competitors," and a 2 for "more than competitors." These can be subjective assessments, just as in the stand-alone risk intelligence score. In general, the scores should vary across different projects, with the possible exception of the record-keeping element. The sum of the answers for the five elements scores your risk intelligence for the main risk of each project.

Risk diversification

The diversification score for the main risk of each project takes the form of a multiple-choice question. Place an *x* beside the most appropriate of the four possible answers.

- Choose the first alternative if the project risk correlates highly with the rest of the risks in the risk strategy. This would be the choice, for example, if Microsoft were evaluating a new office application in the context of all its other office programs. Mathematically, this corresponds to a correlation coefficient of around two-thirds between the main risk of the project and the aggregate of all the risks in the strategy.

- Choose the next alternative if the project risk correlates only a little with the rest of the risks in the risk strategy. This might be the choice if Microsoft were evaluating something as different from most of its products as software for cell phones. Mathematically, it corresponds to a correlation coefficient of about one-third between project risk and total risk.

- Choose the third alternative if the project risk is uncorrelated with the rest of the risks in the risk strategy. This could be the right choice if Microsoft were evaluating a sudden redirection into credit cards. Mathematically, it reflects a correlation coefficient of 0.

- Choose the fourth alternative if the project risk tends to result in positive surprises when the rest of the risks in the strategy are yielding negative surprises, and vice versa. An Internet services provider initiative might possibly be an example of this for Microsoft, on the theory that the fortunes of such providers rise and fall when the fortunes of desktop applications are falling and rising. It reflects a correlation coefficient that's negative.

If enough historical data is available on project results, you can measure diversification as the inverse of project risk correlation coefficients. The correlation coefficient of a project risk with the total risk of a company or division will usually fall between 0 and 1, where 1 reflects perfect correlation. The inverse of this number will usually fall between 1 and 10, where higher values reflect greater diversification. This makes it easy to compare with risk intelligence, which also falls between 1 and 10. (But don't forget that you need to leave a little room above "10" for the rare project risk that's negatively correlated with total risk.)

Project size

Size estimates for each project also take the form of multiple-choice questions. In this case, there are five alternatives for ranges reflecting best estimates for the project's share of revenue or resource

FIGURE 4-4

Risk strategy audit tool: inputs

	Project 1	Project 2	Project 3	Project 4	Project 5	Project 6	Project 7	Project 8
Risk intelligence: For each project, put 0 if less than competitors, 1 if same, and 2 if more								
Amount: How often do you acquire information related to the main project risk?	0	2	1	2	2	0	1	0
Relevance: How relevant is the information to the possible causes of the risk?	1	1	0	1	2	0	2	2
Surprise: How improbable does the information tend to be?	2	0	0	2	2	1	2	1
Diversity: How diverse are your sources of information?	0	1	0	0	1	2	2	1
Record keeping: How easy is it for others to use this information?	1	1	1	2	0	0	2	1
Risk intelligence score for the project	4	5	2	7	7	3	9	5
Risk diversification and project size: For each project put an x by the right answer								
Do you expect project returns will almost always rise and fall with total income?		x	x					
Do you expect project returns will sometimes rise and fall with total income?	x				x			
Do you expect rises and falls in project returns and total income will generally be unrelated?				x		x	x	
Do you expect rises and falls in project returns will generally offset those in total income?								x
Risk diversification of the project	4	2	2	6	4	6	6	8

	Project 1	Project 2	Project 3	Project 4	Project 5	Project 6	Project 7	Project 8
Do you expect project returns to account for less than a tenth of total income in two years?				x		x	x	x
Do you expect project returns to account for 10–20% of total income in two years?	x							
Do you expect project returns to account for 20–30% of total income in two years?			x		x			
Do you expect project returns to account for 30–50% of total income in two years?		x						
Do you expect project returns to account for more than half of total income in two years?								
Expected relative project size	**15%**	**40%**	**15%**	**5%**	**15%**	**5%**	**5%**	**5%**

Risk strategy audit tool: portfolio view

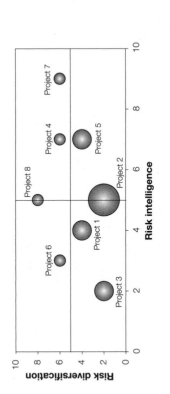

requirements in two years. The ranges are 0–10 percent, 10–20 percent, 20–30 percent, 30–50 percent, or more than 50 percent of total
revenue or resources.

More precise audits

A relatively easy way to raise the objectivity of judgments imbedded
in a risk strategy audit is to survey multiple employees or executives.
Their views on the relative strengths of an organization's risk assessment skills may be more accurate, as a group, than any one person's
view.[3] Beyond this, four of the elements of the risk intelligence score
are quantitative and objectively measurable. In particular, a precise
way to measure relevance appears in the last section of chapter 3.[4]

Even when applied to the major businesses of a company, risk
strategy audits can't provide a full picture of corporate strategy. But
they provide a picture of what corporate strategy most often misses,
namely its risk attributes. Those risk attributes are the flip side of the
growth attributes that most strategies target.

WHO SHOULD CONDUCT RISK STRATEGY AUDITS

Risk strategy audits are appropriate for just about anyone with
a profit and loss (P&L) budget. But their potential application is
a lot broader than that because plenty of people must make tough
resource allocation decisions without having to sign off on a P&L. The
audits are even applicable to choices about major home improvement
projects or a child's after-school activities. Here are some business
examples.

- *Sales and marketing* team leaders and executives can use risk
  strategy audits to allocate sales territories each year with an
  eye to matching individual marketer skills and the closing
  risks in different products or regions. The audits would treat
  each possible marketer/territory combination as a project to

be plotted. They would tend to match high-skill marketers and territories with concentrated closing risks that are likely to yield all-or-nothing results or that are hard for the sales force as a whole to diversify.

- *Operations* leaders and process managers can use risk strategy audits as a part of their quarterly or annual process improvement cycle. The audits will be especially useful in selecting which projects with uncertain outcomes to pursue in-house and which ones to undertake with the help of consultants.

- *Information technology* teams can use risk strategy audits to prioritize risky projects in just the way operations managers can. These audits would use risk intelligence to compare the team's own experience in a problem area with that of potential outside consultants or contractors.

- *Quality control* leaders can use risk strategy audits as part of their annual review of the controls in place for any given operating or financial process. They can support annual Sarbanes-Oxley certification of the adequacy of financial controls as well as annual reviews under the Committee of Sponsoring Organizations (COSO) framework for operating controls. Here audits would treat each potential threat to process quality as a project, evaluating both the process owner's ability to assess any risk not yet mitigated by a control and the extent to which the risk diversifies other process quality threats. The audits should help identify which combination of controls best ensures process quality and efficiency.

- *Procurement* officers can use risk strategy audits to evaluate vendors on an ongoing basis. These audits would treat each potential vendor as a project and would need to reinterpret risk intelligence and diversification to evaluate them. They could treat risk intelligence as the company's familiarity with a given vendor compared with other buyers. And they could treat diversification as the extent to which a vendor increases the company's flexibility. Together, the two factors measure how well the company is likely to manage each vendor and how dependent on each it is becoming.

- *Research and development* teams should use risk strategy audits for annual reassessments of the balance of the risks in their new-product pipelines. The audits can distinguish healthy diversification from distracting fragmentation in the research effort.

- *Legal, compliance, and audit* teams can use risk strategy audits quarterly or annually to determine which of their firms' operating and reputation risks they must mitigate. An example of mitigation might be preempting a safety concern by preventing customers from using a potentially risky product casually. Here, once again, risk intelligence refers to a company's ability to assess any part of a given risk that is not yet mitigated. Risks for which the firm has good intelligence may not require as much preemptive mitigation.

- *Chief financial officers, controllers, and treasurers* can use risk strategy audits to illustrate how their business strategy manages earnings volatility in annual investor and rating agency presentations. Here, each business unit is treated as a project.

- *General managers and corporate strategists*, of course, can apply risk strategy audits directly to their new business development options. This is the most fundamental application of the audits, so let's look at it in more detail.

HOW RISK STRATEGY AUDITS COMPLEMENT
THE BCG GROWTH-SHARE MATRIX

In the late 1970s and early 1980s, the Boston Consulting Group grew to the point that it challenged McKinsey's predominance in strategy consulting and very nearly caught up with it. BCG's not-so-secret weapon was its growth-share matrix. The idea was that you could gauge every line of business in your company—for that matter, you could gauge every project sitting on a shelf at home in your garage—by the attractiveness of the line or project and your relative skills at it. BCG used market growth as a simple measure for attractiveness. For relative skills or competence, BCG used market share on the theory that more share often means lower per-unit cost.

BCG's idea of characterizing a firm's lines of business in terms of the growth of their sectors and the firm's share of their markets is still illuminating. It lets you track the natural life cycles of lines of business. Kodak's film business serves as a good example of how market growth and market share help trace one of these life cycles.

Kodak's film business started as a gelatin dry-plate venture that represented a tiny share of a high-growth but amorphous photo-chemical market. Spurred by its own introduction of handheld folding cameras, the firm's film business took off, and for the better part of a century, it enjoyed decent growth and dominant market share. In time, Japanese competitors eroded Kodak's share of the film market even as the market's growth slowed down. Now, Kodak is letting its share in photochemical paper dwindle to focus on digital and information imaging. Throughout this cycle, film has continually shifted its role in Kodak's overall business portfolio.

BCG helped its clients envision any collection of businesses as a similar portfolio with different combinations of market growth and share. The idea was to invest in the ones where you could become a market leader; milk the ones you already led that were slowing down; and avoid the ones you didn't lead that weren't growing.

But growth is only half the story of the attractiveness of a line of business or project. Risk is the other half, and it is long past time to think through the life cycle of the risks embraced in our major initiatives. The picture of risk strategy generated by a risk strategy audit completes the picture of growth strategy in a growth-share matrix.

Let's look at pictures of a growth strategy and a risk strategy side by side (see figure 4-5). They share three things: our skills relative to competitors matter; our initiatives have a natural pattern of evolution; and we must think about filling the pipeline.

The scales to the left of both grids measure aspects of our initiatives that are largely uncontrollable: the extent to which they diversify our risks and the growth of their underlying markets. But the horizontal scales measure something we partly control: our ability to assess the risks and our share of the market. This is the dial we must move for each initiative as it moves through the grid. All things being equal, we'd rather be in the upper-right cell of both. But nothing stays still on these strategy grids.

The movement of initiatives tends to follow very similar patterns on both. We've already discussed it for a risk strategy matrix. But one of the crucial insights of the original growth-share matrix was that initiatives, lines of business, and projects follow a natural pattern of market growth and market share. New initiatives are often in high-growth sectors (upper left). We invest in them to grow our market

FIGURE 4-5

Risk strategy matrix versus growth strategy matrix

share (upper right). Over time, the market slows down (lower right). Eventually we divest (lower left).

Ideally, we will always have an initiative with an attractive combination of growth and share on the growth grid. And we will always have an initiative where our risk intelligence and the risk's diversity are both high. To ensure this, we must keep our pipeline of initiatives filled. When white spaces appear along the top of either grid, it's time to think about what new projects we should explore.

But however these pictures of growth or risk strategies may appear, it's dangerous to allocate resources or prioritize initiatives based on either one of them alone. This is exactly what most venture capitalists in the technology sector did through 2001.

The typical venture capital portfolio had an irresistible growth strategy, and the growth-share matrix for any one of them would have shown it. These investments were in the Internet and in software, the highest growth sectors around. And because of the proliferation of business models applying the Internet or computing power to older sectors, many of these investments dominated their budding markets.

What no one analyzed was the risk strategy imbedded in these venture capital portfolios. The risk strategy matrix for any one of them would have shown a picture as grim as the growth strategy appeared bright (see figure 4-6). Since these portfolios were not

FIGURE 4-6

Typical venture capital growth and risk strategies (circa 2000)

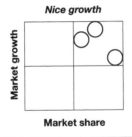

diversified, their investments would have clustered at the bottom of a risk strategy matrix. And since many of these technologists were taking on entrenched "old economy" competitors, they had to bear nontechnology risks their competitors understood better. So the risks huddled in the lower-left cell. This is the crash position, and crash is what happened.

THE FOUR SEASONS OF RISK STRATEGY PATTERNS

If this theory of risk pipelines is right, then the healthiest risk strategies are the ones that appear balanced, without major holes, on a risk strategy matrix. There are two possible types. One type would be a company in "reap and sow" mode with a concentrated exposure to a business it knows well plus lots of smaller experiments. Microsoft might be an example. Its matrix would show a major initiative in the cell for high risk intelligence and low diversification (see figure 4-7).

Another type would be a company in "nurture" mode with growing exposure to a business it is beginning to dominate as it phases out some older ones. Apple and its ubiquitous iPods would be a great example. Its matrix would show a major initiative in the cell for high risk intelligence and high diversification (see figure 4-7).

FIGURE 4-7

Reap-and-sow versus nurture strategies

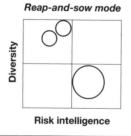 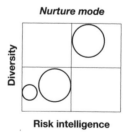

Strategies with characteristic weak spots show up clearly, too. In fact, it's possible to put every lopsided risk strategy with a large hole somewhere in the pipeline in one of four buckets, depending on the position of the hole. This is a simplification, but it tells you a lot about what to do to make sure a balanced risk strategy underlies your company's business portfolio—or even your personal project portfolio.

Call the strategies with characteristic weak spots "winter," "spring," "summer," and "fall" strategies. Each strategy pattern corresponds to the position of its risk strategy hole. The seasons are a mnemonic device, following the characteristic holes they name clockwise around a risk strategy matrix. Here are some working definitions:

- *Winter strategy:* little dominance (no major initiatives with high risk intelligence)

- *Spring strategy:* little focus (no major initiatives with low diversification)

- *Summer strategy:* little development (few experimental initiatives with low risk intelligence)

- *Fall strategy:* little resilience (few initiatives with high diversification)

Winter strategies

Winter strategies are risk strategies with little dominance.

Winter strategies

New companies often have winter pattern risk strategies. However dynamic their management teams and however well designed their business plans, they rarely have access to as much relevant, high-impact information as entrenched competitors. So their initiatives would show up to the left of a risk strategy matrix. They try to overcome this disadvantage through innovation and energetic execution.

Well-established companies can easily revert to a winter strategy, too. Diversified technology companies are especially prone to it because it is so hard to stay abreast of change in many markets at once. For example, Sony Corporation currently finds itself in a winter pattern. The video-game market is too dynamic for any player to hope to maintain risk assessment advantages in it. Nor has Sony kept up with smaller firms like Apple in consumer electronics and technologists like Matsushita in TV screens. And it has never seemed adept in creative content sectors. Consequently, its businesses diversify the company to varying degrees but lack dominant risk intelligence positions.

There is an analogy between risk strategies reflecting gaps in what we might call a company's *learning life cycle* and common biases in our personal learning styles. For example, students who dabble in activities without mastering them resemble winter strategy firms. It can be exhilarating to the extent new challenges are stimulating, but over time dilettantism's disappointing results are discouraging. Most of us must devote enough time to at least one activity to enjoy some success in it.

The remedy for a winter strategy company or division is no different from the winter strategy student's. Invest in a promising initiative and develop expertise and habits and capabilities of learning about its uncertainties inferior to none. This will often transform a risk strategy pattern from winter to spring.

Spring strategies

Spring strategies are risk strategies with little focus.

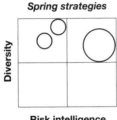

The risk strategies of conglomerates often follow a spring pattern because, regardless of their expertise in specific business areas, their risks are diverse. Consequently, their business units and initiatives fall in the upper half of a risk strategy matrix. Since it reduces total or entity risk, diversification can be a good thing. The problem is that firms often pursue it at the expense of developing expertise or learning capabilities in specific risks. They end up merely replicating what their investors can do more easily.

Sometimes diversification can actually signal a weakness. While Nestlé has been successful throughout the world, for example, its brands and country organizations have grown to the point where they lack coherence. This allows for great flexibility in both product planning and market strategy. But it prevents the firm from putting the full weight of its global name, talent, and resources behind critical opportunities. Nestlé enjoys the spring strategy's benefit of being hostage to no one product or market. But the firm is working hard to develop more of a center of gravity.

A student pursuing widely scattered activities may similarly reflect a spring strategy. This can be a sign of healthy wonder at the world but also the mark of someone who is afraid to focus. For companies as well as students, diversity is a great way to manage risk unless it masks an unwillingness to select and pursue major opportunities.

Spring strategy companies that want to increase their focus almost invariably funnel their resources into the highest-growth areas where they enjoy high risk intelligence. This increases their exposure to a narrow set of risks, but they are risks the company understands by definition better than most. Those who succeed transform their risk strategies from spring to summer.

Summer strategies

Summer strategies are strategies with little development.

Summer strategies

Diversity

Risk intelligence

Companies whose risk strategies show a summer pattern usually dominate their business segments. Whether they're high- or low-growth firms, they tend to be conservative in choosing where to compete. They stick to their knitting, and only the stuff they knit best. But this raises the question of what will replace their businesses if despite how well they understand those businesses their markets become unprofitable. On a risk strategy matrix, their business lines fall to the right, with very little in the way of low risk intelligence experiments on the left.

While this risk pattern is vulnerable to reversals in its main markets, companies whose risk strategies reflect it are often at the top of their game. Wal-Mart Stores, for example, consistently ranks as one of *Fortune*'s Most Admired Companies. The firm is an acknowledged world leader in most of its business activities. But it may now be becoming a victim of its own success.

Wal-Mart's efforts to grow into new countries and U.S. urban areas are creating unprecedented friction over local land development and workforce unionization and compensation. This is attracting unwelcome political attention. A 2004 report by Representative George Miller (D-CA), for example, argues federal support for the company's low-paid staff cost the public over $2,000 per person annually.[5]

So why does it continue to push into areas where people resist large stores or take unions more seriously? The problem is that Wal-Mart has not really experimented with other ways to compete. Doing so would have meant lines of business like specialty stores, where the company never developed expertise or extraordinary learning capabilities. But it would have created growth options.

Children with specific athletic, artistic, or intellectual gifts illustrate the summer strategy bias in personal learning. They focus on what they do well and learn quickly. But when do you urge a child to go for it, to become a concert pianist or an all-star track-and-field athlete? After all, a bad tendon or a change in artistic taste can seriously derail an emerging prodigy. The problem is not just that we all should have backup plans. It's that lucky summer strategy children, rather like the natural successes of the corporate world that struck a good business plan and never looked back, must *learn how to learn things* that may not come easily to them. Exploration can be hard for prodigies.

Summer strategy companies must force themselves not to rest on their laurels. Nobody else will do so: certainly not shareholders, who are enjoying the ride and can sell when it's over; certainly not customers who are well served; and certainly not board leadership responsible for the firm's successful focus. Change must come from the operating leaders who want to put their own stamp on something.

Fall strategies

Fall strategies are risk strategies with little resilience.

Fall strategies

The fall strategy company is in trouble, and a traditional analysis of its growth and market shares will not show it. The threat lies in its business risks. The fall pattern in a company's risk strategy reflects risks that, however well it understands them, are overconcentrated. Even novices can attack it because, as argued earlier, they can finance themselves cheaply as long as their experiments are small and diversified.

While analysts have written many premature reports of General Motors's death, its risk strategy fits the fall pattern. The sheer breadth of its markets should guarantee diversity. But the company's profits have recently relied heavily on its sales of larger vehicles, including sports utility vehicles. A reversal in the U.S. tax or licensing treatment of these vehicles would wreak havoc with most analysts' profit forecasts for the whole company. What it lacks are profit generators not subject to those risks.

The analogous fall strategy child is one who becomes one-sided without the summer strategy child's preeminent passion to justify it. The danger here is not so much forgetting how to learn as the possibility of neglecting an undiscovered passion. Fall strategies are a sign that a child or a company has stopped developing new interests.

Fall strategy firms generally must restart their internal business development engines. This is a risk pattern that can justify diversification at the expense of risk intelligence because diversification is what it lacks. In many cases, however, it will be possible to diversify into areas where the organization has some risk assessment advantages. We've already seen Pfizer do this.

But a more broadly applicable remedy is expansion into places that are geographically and behaviorally remote from the home market. Look for investments in markets like China as a response to the threats underlying a fall risk strategy.

This is an exception to the tendency of risk intelligence, as a strategic consideration, to weigh against business diversification. The final section, for example, considers risk intelligence as a guardrail against unprincipled diversification. Also trading on the dynamics of diversification, "Risk and the Business Cycle" asks if the dynamics of risk intelligence can help explain sticky wages and recessions.

ACQUISITIONS AND UNPRINCIPLED DIVERSIFICATION

The most important business application of risk strategy audits may be in acquisition planning. Corporate development in general—and corporate acquisitions in particular—suffers from the fact that we focus on what we can measure. When it comes to the risks in acquiring a target, what we can measure is their correlation to the major risks we're already managing. But that can lead to overvaluing diversification. It's already a bias in companies that feel the pressure to grow. When you add the pressure for growth to the fact that diversification is the only easily measured risk attribute in most acquisition targets, *unprincipled diversification results.*

Risk strategy audits provide a long-needed antidote to unprincipled diversification in corporate development. By explicitly measuring a firm's likelihood of mastering the risks underlying a particular acquisition target, we can integrate the crucial competitive dimension of risk assessment with the benefits of diversification in evaluating alternatives. You don't want to add a business whose risks are too far left on a risk strategy matrix just to extend your risks upward. Companies should not become mutual funds. Risk strategy audits can help them avoid the temptation.

Risk and the Business Cycle

The life cycle of the risks companies tackle as they grow may help explain the business cycle. This is because companies embarking on new initiatives rarely understand the risks involved as well as entrenched competitors. When this is the case, they may be reluctant to negotiate lower wages in a recession. And if companies feel they must pay a new hire the same even when, as in a recession, they may expect lower productivity from the new hire, there will be less hiring, and the recession won't self-correct. The argument breaks into three parts.

First, companies that want to grow into new areas usually have low risk intelligence in the relevant risks. By now you can probably guess why. Different learnable risks have different causes. Different causes require different kinds of learning. And our learning skills are as diverse as the risks we must juggle. So there's no reason to expect to be very good at learning the drivers of the risks behind a new initiative.

Second, and this is the surprising part of the argument, companies growing into areas where they have low risk intelligence may hesitate to lower their compensation offers in a soft labor market. If they understood the risks buffeting results in the new line of business as well as the companies already in it, they would know which candidates can handle the job and which can't. But companies new to the field don't know this, or if they do, they don't trust themselves yet. They worry that offering too little will saddle them with managers who can't learn quickly enough to catch up with market leaders.

For example, suppose you run two restaurants specializing in Finnish food. But you worry that it's a fall strategy because you're overexposed to the risk that folks in town will grow tired of caribou. You decide to diversify by opening a bar even though the economy is slowing down. Your business manager says you can probably get away with offering 80 percent of the going rate for bartenders and hiring five. But you don't know what makes for a good bartender, so you sure don't want to scare away the best candidates in the market. Consequently, you decide to hire just four at the normal rate.

The third part of the argument is straightforward. In a recession, firms' resources can't produce as much as they can when the economy is growing fast. If they could, it wouldn't be a recession. But if they decide to pay as much for certain new hires in a recession when those hires are less productive, they'll make fewer of that kind of hires.

It turns out that these are precisely the kind of hires that seem to matter in recessions. New evidence shows job loss stays surprisingly constant in recessions.[6] What slows down is hiring as a percent of job seekers. It's probably fair to speculate that companies try to fill vacancies in old positions internally during a recession. If so, the evidence suggests that something keeps compensation offers for new employees from adjusting downward when more people are looking for work.

Employers new to a business may fear their low relative risk intelligence puts them at a disadvantage in using a soft market to hire more job seekers. They may especially fear hiring people at salary levels lower than companies already in the business paid before the soft market.

So why don't companies that already know the business use their high relative risk intelligence to exploit that soft market? It may be because their existing employees will probably work harder to secure their prerecession salaries. If so, they would have fairness problems negotiating soft-market salaries with lower trajectories for new hires.

(continued)

This implies that employers don't drive hard bargains in soft markets when they fear others may understand the market better than they do. In other words, it implies that employer fears arising from at least primitive intuitions about risk intelligence may account for the business cycle. And in more traditional economic terms, it suggests that information asymmetries—not between employers and job seekers but between employers and competitors in new business areas—may explain the "sticky wages" that cause cyclical unemployment.

How might one tell whether this view of a possible role of risk intelligence in business cycles is right? It implies that you won't necessarily find big boom-and-bust cycles in economies with little growth in risky new areas. But you would find those cycles in economies growing in areas requiring new resources, types of labor, technology, or know-how. So on this view, sticky wages arise not so much from the nature of labor agreements in heavily capitalized economies. They arise from employers' awareness and fears of what they might not know as well others.

Building Networks That Can Adapt to Risk

The last two chapters showed that learnable risks pose a real problem. Do we face barriers that will keep us from learning as much as others about the learnable risks in a new area? Or do they face barriers that will keep them from learning as much as we will? The problem arises precisely because our technology is starting to help us track what we learn about practical risks. It matters because we could be choosing initiatives where we have real risk learning disadvantages that will keep us from succeeding.

Part of the solution is to have a view on *which* learnable risks we're likely to understand and track better over time than others can. Of two risky alternatives with similar expected returns, we should prefer the one where we enjoy a risk intelligence advantage. But there's got to be more to it. After all, no company is an island, to borrow the phrase, any more than any person is. How should our business and personal *networks* affect the way we think about risk?

Specifically, do our networks change which risky alternatives we should prefer when we have a choice? And are there different roles within those networks that can help us, and them, better absorb our risks?

Networks make us look beyond ourselves. Of course, learnable risks have forced us to compare the capabilities of competitors. But there are also tactical advantages in understanding the needs of potential partners.

This chapter proposes a tool, the risk-role matrix, for thinking about what role in our business and personal networks best handles different kinds of risks. An important feature of the tool is that it suggests different roles for different kinds of random risks as well as for different kinds of learnable ones. This is the first time we've seen systematic advantages and disadvantages in handling random risks. The reason is that networks can help us not only assess risks, but also manage and absorb them, persistently better.

Risk-role matrices raise the issue of what kinds of pitfalls surround random risks. After all, most of our projects, initiatives, and decisions involve both random and learnable risks. It's urgent because questions about our ability to handle risks arise in every investor call and every board of directors presentation on growth strategies.

As businesses in the United States, Europe, and Japan increasingly recognize that most of the world's future growth will come from emerging markets, they are starting to grapple with dauntingly unfamiliar risks. Is it good news or bad when unfamiliar risks are also random? The perspective of risk networks helps provide an answer.

This chapter argues that differences in our natural networks for absorbing certain risks can create lasting advantages in businesses subject to them. This is especially true if we think through the best roles we can play in those networks. And for once, it's as true of random risks as it is of learnable risks. The fourth rule sums it up:

Rule 1. Recognize which risks are learnable.

Rule 2. Identify risks you can learn about fastest.

Rule 3. Sequence risky projects in a "learning pipeline."

Rule 4. Keep networks of partners to manage all risks.

NETWORKS AND OUR RISK ECOLOGY

Earlier chapters of *Risk Intelligence* have direct implications for dealing with unfamiliar risks. Break up projects into challenges involving learnable and random risks. Then create a pipeline of learnable risks you can master faster than others can.

The problem for learnable risks is that sometimes you have to bear one that you will never understand as well as the competition. So the question for learnable risks is whether you can build a network to help handle it and offset your disadvantage.

When it comes to random risks that no one can assess better than anyone else, you can follow these rules to the letter and still lose out to someone who is better at marshaling support. The question of whether you can build a network with a *systematic* risk management advantage is especially important for random risks since learning speed makes no difference. The most stable differentiating factor may be our allies.[1]

But not just any allies. The kinds of risks that block great growth opportunities require more than a casual partner or two. They demand a network of people and companies with a reason to take up our cause, whether it involves helping to protect us or being protected by us. Unless your ranks of loyal friends are limitless, you need to determine what kind of network will come together around a risk and what kind of role you should play in it. The answers depend on the nature of the risk and how your and other people's exposure to it develops. Two *risk-role factors* drive this exposure.

The first factor is how well you can diversify the exposure. For example, you may be evaluating whether your company should buy a tech start-up involved in fuel cells. Fuel cells require hydrogen. But you have no way to predict the rising and falling price of hydrogen that may affect the start-up's success. That price is a random factor that you have no way of determining. But it may still offset gains and losses from your other businesses. So you should determine how much the risk in hydrogen prices offsets or diversifies other risks you face.

The second factor is the breadth of exposure to the risk. Suppose, for example, that other companies are starting to buy fuel cell technology as well. Then exposure to hydrogen price risk may become more widespread in the economy. You still have to worry about how much volatility the risk in hydrogen prices will add to your earnings. But now you also have to think about whether it will add similar volatility to the earnings of lots of other firms—firms that never had such an exposure before.

If more firms' earnings become sensitive to swings in hydrogen prices, investors won't be able to avoid the risk in those prices so easily by diversifying their investments. And that means your investors will grow sensitive to the hydrogen price risk in your earnings, too. They'll need higher returns because they can no longer diversify the risk.

Together, these two risk-role factors define the position of a project, initiative, or personal decision in the broader risk ecology of the person or firm facing a choice. By *risk ecology*, I mean just the network of customers, suppliers, colleagues, family members, competitors, allies, and other counterparties affected by related risks. A project's position in its risk ecology, then, depends on the value of the two risk-role factors for the principal risk or risks underlying the project or initiative.

Call the first factor *diversifiability*. Projects with high diversifiability put you in a position to absorb risk from counterparties in your risk ecology. For example, if most of your risks reflect uncertainty in economic growth but not in commodity prices, then a project subject to risk from hydrogen prices (a commodity) will diversify your overall risk. You may even be in a better position to absorb that risk from suppliers or customers with whom you want to do business involving hydrogen-based risk. Diversifiability should be familiar by now because it played a role in the risk strategy audits of chapter 4.

The second factor, however, is new. It reflects how much of a project's risks correlate with broad measures of the stock market. Call the second factor *market intensity.* Projects with high market intensity will have to earn higher returns. This is because investors cannot diversify the market-correlated component of a project's risk.

Here's another example to help make the concept of market intensity more concrete. Suppose I have two projects: selling customized cars and building a revolutionary new wind sock. The car project is probably highly dependent on economic growth and thus has a lot of market-correlated risk. The wind sock project is risky, but the connection with overall market risk appears small. The car project will probably have to earn higher returns because of its market intensity. Its returns are more likely to rise and fall in line with the other exposures of anyone investing in it.

Let's try to picture how risky projects fit into risk ecologies. We'll want to see how these two factors of diversifiability and market intensity relate to one another and why they matter to the risk networks we build.

USING RISK-ROLE MATRICES TO MANAGE RISK THROUGH NETWORKS

The kind of partners or support network you need to help absorb the risks in a potentially valuable project will depend on the factors of diversifiability and market intensity. Diversifiability reflects how well your firm's other projects diversify the risk; market intensity is a function of how many other firms are taking a risk like it.

Figure 5-1 shows the role you should play in a network of partners that can help manage risks with any combination of these two factors. It applies to any kind of risk. But for random risks, risk roles may be the only lasting source of advantage.

Projects whose risks you or your organization can diversify against other risks you already bear fall in the upper row. Those you cannot, fall below. If this sounds familiar, it should: it's just like the risk strategy matrix from the last chapter. And just as with the risk strategy matrix, risk-role matrices are specific to your or your organization's risks. Others might have to place a similar project elsewhere.

What is new are the columns. They no longer depend on the concept of risk intelligence but rather the extent to which the risk in question pervades the economy.

Projects whose principal learnable or random risks are largely uncorrelated with the overall market fall in the left column. More specifically, the market-related component of these risks is small. So these risks are only weakly related to the rise and fall of the securities market as a whole. For example, a project subject to weather risk would probably fall in the left column because the relationship between the weather and overall market performance is tenuous. If many firms did have similar exposure to one of these risks, the

FIGURE 5-1

Risk-role matrix

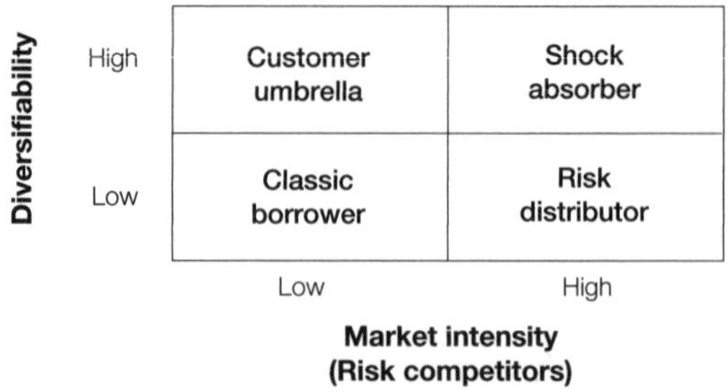

		Market intensity (Risk competitors)	
		Low	High
Diversifiability	High	Customer umbrella	Shock absorber
	Low	Classic borrower	Risk distributor

market would start to reflect it, and its market intensity would increase.

Naturally, projects whose risks are more widely shared would fall in the right column. After all, if more firms share an exposure, the market will start to reflect it in the sense that overall market risk will start to correlate with it. For example, projects subject to the health of the overall economy would tend to fall to the right since the risk is widely shared and directly correlated with overall market movements.

The risk-role matrix helps you think about risk partners because it situates you or your organization in the larger ecology of the risks each of your projects bears. It emphasizes roles you or your organization can play based on the diversifiability and market intensity of the major risks in any major project or initiative you're evaluating.

The implications of diversifiability are fairly intuitive. You should probably find partners who need help with project risks you can diversify. And you should probably seek partners who can help bear project risks you cannot diversify.

The implications of market intensity are a little less intuitive. Project risks with low market intensity are likely to reflect supply-side uncertainties. For example, a soft drinks firm may try out a new formula. There's little organic connection between risk around the popularity of the new formula and risk around the growth of the economy. So risk underlying the new formula's success, a pure supply-side risk, has low market intensity. The example also illustrates the fact that customers—restaurants and grocery stores, in this example—may need protection from supply-side risks. The risks of projects to the left of a risk-role matrix are often hardest on customers.

Similarly, project risks with high market correlation are likely to reflect demand-side risks. Consider, for example, a company that supplies sweetener for all of the soft drinks firm's products. If customers feel pinched from a weak economy, and they cut back on soft drinks in favor of water, the supplier suffers. The general principle seems to be that suppliers often need protection from marketwide risks. So risks on the right side of a risk-role matrix are often hardest on suppliers.

Risk-role matrices indicate favorable roles for each combination of risk diversifiability and market intensity in a project. Let's call them *customer umbrella, classic borrower, shock absorber,* and *risk distributor,* and take them up in turn along with a note on measurement (see "Risk-Role Measures").

CUSTOMER UMBRELLAS

Suppose your division operates a chain of hardware stores. It's looking at an initiative whose main risks you can easily diversify and not many other firms share. For example, your division may want to outsource the parts supply–ordering process to a provider who can help keep store inventory down while monitoring purchasing to avoid running out of anything (stock-outs). The quality of the provider represents an idiosyncratic risk that you can diversify and few others face.

Since the diversifiability of the risk puts it in the top part of the risk-role matrix and its low market intensity puts it on the left, the initiative falls in the upper-left cell (see figure 5-1). The matrix indicates your division is in a position to play the risk role of *customer umbrella.* Basically, you can afford to protect your customers from risk due to the new supplier and perhaps in exchange retain more of the advantages of the outsourcing arrangement.

The reason is that your ability to diversify the risk lets you absorb it more easily, all things being equal, than your customers, other suppliers, and other partners. But where in the larger risk ecology of the initiative does the risk arise, and who's subject to it?

The risk from outsourcing the ordering process is probably unrelated to overall market movements. After all, it doesn't reflect changes in market demand or customer appetite, and few other firms share

Risk-Role Measures

How can you measure diversifiability and market intensity? Estimating "more" or "less" is often enough for a useful risk-role matrix. But even a more precise estimate can be fairly straightforward.

Find data going back five or six years for the profit margin of projects like the one you're considering, the profit margin of your business, and the returns of a major stock market index like the S&P 500. You'll also need two pieces of graph paper.

To determine diversifiability, plot the business and project profit margins for each year of data. To plot a point for any year of data, measure the profit margin of your business along the horizontal axis and the profit margin of the project along the vertical.

If the dots fall in a neat line, the project's diversifiability is low for your business. The project should appear low on a risk-role matrix. If the dots fall in a rough line, the diversifiability is a little higher but still below the middle line of the matrix. If the dots fall in an oblong patch, the diversifiability is fairly high, and the project should be just above the matrix's middle line. If the dots are widely scattered, the diversifiability is high, and the project should appear near the top of the matrix (see figure 5-2).

To determine market intensity, plot market index returns and project profit margins for each year of data. For any year, measure

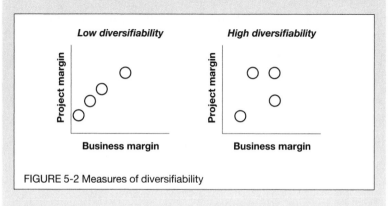

FIGURE 5-2 Measures of diversifiability

the returns on a marketwide index along the horizontal axis and the profit margin of the project along the vertical.

If the dots fall in a neat line, the project's market intensity is high and it would have what is sometimes called a high *Sharpe ratio*.[2] The project should appear to the right on a risk-role matrix. If the dots fall in a rough line, the market intensity is a little lower but still to the right of middle line of the matrix. If the dots fall in an oblong patch, the market intensity is fairly low, and the project should be just to the left of the matrix's middle line. If the dots are widely scattered, the market intensity is low and the project should appear to the left of the matrix (see figure 5-3).

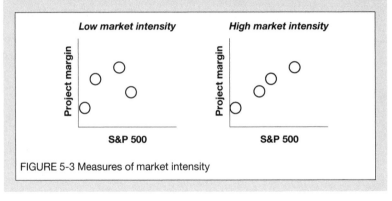

FIGURE 5-3 Measures of market intensity

it. If the provider served many other firms, and if its services were critically important, then the risk might show some correlation with the market. But that's not the case here. If we had to say that the risk arises more from customers or suppliers, we would say it arises from suppliers.

This makes plenty of sense in the case of outsourcing. It also makes sense that it's your customers, if anyone, who need protection from the risks introduced by your decision to outsource the ordering process. Furthermore, your division is in a position to absorb exactly that risk. So you should act as a customer umbrella.

This corresponds to any initiative or investment where the risk is not too correlated with the rest of your firm's major business risks (which lets you diversify it) and not too correlated with the risks of other companies in the market (which means customers will try to avoid it). In these cases, the initiative or investment probably won't raise your cost of capital very much even if you absorb all the risk. Moreover, by absorbing the risk and protecting your customers from it, you may win better pricing from them.

In the case of the hardware parts–ordering provider, for example, you might offer customers cash discounts on any parts that one of your stores has to special-order because of a stock-out. If the provider is helping the stores trim cost, there should be some level of discount that will be attractive to customers while generating savings for the division.

In short, you may want to consider acting as a customer umbrella, protecting your customers from initiatives with diversifiable, idiosyncratic risks. But what should you do if you cannot diversify those idiosyncratic risks?

CLASSIC BORROWERS

If you are less able to diversify a project's risk, but there still aren't many others exposed to it, the role you should consider is that of *classic borrower*, in the lower-left cell of the risk-role matrix (see figure 5-1). These are the situations where financing from a bank or an investment group able to bear risk is probably most beneficial.

Let's say we decide to launch a new business for dog owners called Slobber Stick. The idea is a crucial variation on the plastic stick-and-ball sets that dog owners use to play catch with their pets on a walk. We think we've got a technology that will let the stick pick up any old ball a dog may happen to adore. The question is about the nature of Slobber Stick's risks; what kind of network of business partners, suppliers, and customers we should build to manage those risks; and what role we should play in it.

Let's say Slobber Stick is our only venture, so we can't really diversify its risks. That means Slobber Stick will fall in the lower half of the risk-role matrix.

But what kind of risks are we looking at? There's technology risk. Will the stick work with high-slobber dogs and high-slobber balls? There's also design risk. How big is the slobber-sensitive part of the dog-owner market? And there's competitive risk. Are dog owners losing the plastic balls from their existing stick-and-ball sets as fast as I lose golf balls? There doesn't seem to be a large market-correlated component to these risks. If that's right, we're in the lower-left corner of the risk-role matrix.

The upshot is that we face business risks that we *can't* diversify but that a diversified investor *can* diversify. These are the kinds of risks for which banks and venture capital firms were made. We should find a financial partner.

Because a diversified financial partner will be able to diversify Slobber Stick's business risks, we can expect affordable funding. It may be hard to borrow since our inability to diversify the risks raises the threat of bankruptcy if things don't go well. But we may be able to find equity investors, given their ability to diversify low market-intensity risks and a product most customers will drool over.

In sum, a project with idiosyncratic risks that you can't diversify cries out for a financial partner. The partner's ability to diversify the risks lets the partner borrow against the investment even if you cannot. The opposite situation provides a dramatic risk-role contrast: diversifiable risks that correlate with the market.

SHOCK ABSORBERS

Once again, we're looking at projects or initiatives with risks you can diversify. The difference here is that you're no longer alone in facing those risks. More precisely, the risks correlate with rises and falls in the overall stock market. Projects with risks you can diversify that have a large market-related component fall in the upper-right cell (see figure 5-1). With projects like these, you should consider playing the role of *shock absorber* in your network of partners, customers, and suppliers. In a nutshell, you can protect suppliers and partners from market-generated shocks.

Before we work through an example, it's worth taking a look at the rates of return investors will expect for bearing these kinds of risk. Every project that a company undertakes imposes risk on its investors through the volatility of the project's contribution to company profits. The surprising thing is that you may need astronomical rates of return on shock absorber projects to stay involved. There are two reasons.

First, since the risks of this kind of project are fairly widespread, most investors will not be able to diversify them. They will thus need higher rates of return. So you will have to squeeze higher returns out of the project than you might otherwise expect.

Second, the better you can diversify a project's risks, the less the project will contribute to your total risk. And the less it contributes to your overall risk, the more you will be able to borrow to finance any investments it requires. But if you borrow a lot to finance the project, then the company's equity investment in it will become risky because of the project's leverage. The same thing happens, for example, if you have an 80 percent mortgage, and housing prices rise 5 percent: your investment is up 25 percent because of the leverage.

Lots of managers find their companies in just this situation today and cannot figure out why. It's especially true of companies adding "solutions" businesses that surround a core software, hardware, or manufactured product with consulting, advisory, and maintenance services. The point is to tackle more general customer problems. IBM undertook a major solutions initiative when Lou Gerstner took over in 1993.

These solutions businesses have risks that are quite different from the risks of a hardware, software, or manufacturing company, so solutions ventures usually fall in the top half of our grid. But the risks in solutions businesses are highly market correlated. Not only are a lot of firms jumping into these advisory businesses, but their customers' ability to defer consulting projects makes advisory services supersensitive to the overall health of the market. Thus, solutions initiatives have risks that fall in the upper-right cell.

The problem is that while managers don't expect these advisory businesses to eat up a lot of capital, what they do require becomes unbelievably expensive as consulting profits rise and fall with the overall economy. And if you try to run one to cover its costs with a thin layer of profit, even your customers and suppliers will become skeptical about your willingness to support it through a business downturn.

Still, organizations that can diversify these kinds of risks can absorb them and even shield their risk networks from them. Since these risks are by definition market correlated, they often reflect uncertainty in customer demand. That means the diversification capacity of shock absorbers lets them shield suppliers and other partners selling complementary goods and services from market-generated shocks.

For example, if your firm adds solutions consulting and can diversify its risks, you may be able to negotiate very attractive pricing from hardware suppliers whose products work with the systems you are helping your customer build. This will be especially true where you can provide some stability over time to those hardware suppliers' order books. In essence, you're shielding them from the ups and downs of the market in exchange for competitive pricing. To extract full benefit from the partnership, you may incorporate the hardware in your solutions consulting engagement.

In sum, projects with risks you can diversify that are market correlated create opportunities to play the role of shock absorber. Shock absorbers are in a position to shield partners from risks that probably (given their high market correlation) relate to customer demand. But your role changes sharply if you can't diversify these risks.

RISK DISTRIBUTORS

The last kind of risk role is for projects with widely shared risks that you or your organization cannot diversify. The diversification challenge of these projects for your organization puts them in the lower half of the matrix. The large market-related component of the risks, reflecting how broadly companies are subject to them, moves them to the right side. The role you'll need to consider for projects in the lower-right cell (see figure 5-1) is that of the *risk distributor,* because your difficulty in diversifying the risks makes them hard to bear alone. But asking for help with these kinds of risks is asking a lot, because they will exacerbate your partners' undiversifiable exposure to the market.

There are lots of examples of lines of business that demand a risk distributor role. Airlines cannot diversify their exposure to increases and decreases in business travel, for example, and that exposure is highly related to market swings. Since the risk reflects uncertainty about customer behavior, they turn to their suppliers for help in cushioning it. This is why aircraft companies like Boeing and Airbus frequently let airlines opt out of purchase agreements.

Store and restaurant franchise operators also face hard-to-diversify market risks that they need help absorbing. Category retailers often help their store operators bear market-related risks by letting them return unsold inventory. And retailers like Wal-Mart, with a lot of negotiating leverage, often push risk back on their suppliers.

It's not always a zero-sum game, however. If you face market-related risks that you cannot diversify, you should look for shock absorbers in your supply chain or among other business partners like those selling complementary products. Risk distributors who partner with shock absorbers may be highly competitive as a team. In fact, they can enjoy risk-based advantages as a team even where they don't have distinct individual advantages. What really matters is your network's success in meeting end-customer needs. If you can build a winning risk network, then the suppliers and sellers in your network will find mutually profitable prices for the services and parts that go into the end product.

LONE WOLVES, DABBLERS, AND RISK-ROLE MIGRATION

Risk-role matrices don't reveal revolutionary forces driving the evolution of project risks quite the way risk strategy matrices do. But they capture forces at work on project and decision risks that have an impact on what challenges we should tackle and how to organize for them.

For one thing, just as in the case of risk strategy matrices and the learnable risks they track, projects on a risk-role matrix will tend to fall if they're successful. The reason is that if a project or an initiative succeeds, it will have a bigger impact on your or your organization's overall results. That means that its risks will become harder for you to diversify. Projects with less diversifiable risks appear lower on the matrix (see figure 5-4).

Moreover, as lines of business mature, they will migrate to the right of the matrix. Not too long ago, for example, businesses subject

FIGURE 5-4

Project migration on a risk-role matrix

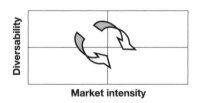

Market intensity

to uncertainty about the growth of Internet acceptance had risk with little correlation to the overall market. As the Internet spread, it became harder to find any business that was not subject to uncertainty about Internet usage. Internet-related risks correlate with the market because Internet businesses are now a significant part of the market.

As a result, successful projects and initiatives will tend to migrate to the right and down on most organizations' risk-role matrices. That means your risk role may well change over time from customer umbrella (upper left) to risk distributor (lower right).

This fits nicely with intuition. When we start something completely new, we need to make it as easy and risk free for our new customers as possible. We play the role of customer umbrella. Eventually, as our time and resource investment grows, we reach a point where we need to pass the risks of a maturing project or business to suppliers who have benefited from the market we've helped build. We become risk distributors.

Automobile manufacturing is a good example of a mature industry whose risks are highly concentrated in the major firms and strongly correlated with the market. It's no surprise that they need to distribute some of the risk they bear to parts suppliers like Delphi and Valeo. But once upon a time, the Model T sold at a price ($300) that all but eliminated risk to the customer.

Most of the time, though, our projects and therefore our risk roles fall between the early days, when we act as customer umbrellas, and the later days, when we become risk distributors. Which path will our projects or initiatives take? Will they take the "high road" through the upper-right cell for shock absorbers? Or will they take the "low road" through the lower-left cell for classic borrowers?

It depends on which is growing faster: the share of our total revenues contributed by the project or the share of total economic activity similar projects generate.

Low road

For example, if we launch an initiative around new, hydrogen-based fuel cells in an energy company, the company could well devote itself to the new technology before it becomes widely accepted. So for a time, it would be hard for the company to diversify the venture's risk, but the risk wouldn't be strongly market related (see figure 5-5). This is the low road: the company should play the role of the classic borrower.

High road

On the other hand, we might launch a fuel cell initiative in an auto company. Here it's unlikely that the initiative would ever dominate the firm's business. Hydrogen-based energy would start to have an impact on the economy long before fuel cells made much of a contribution to the auto manufacturer's earnings. This company would be

FIGURE 5-5

Low-road risk-role migration path

FIGURE 5-6

High-road risk-role migration path

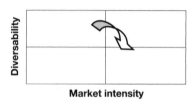

on the high road in the growing market for fuel cells. It should probably play the role of shock absorber in the emerging hydrogen-based risk ecology (see figure 5-6).

Financial constraints and the choice between focusing and dabbling

So the trajectory a project follows depends on whether its diversifiability or market intensity is changing faster. Are a few individuals or groups taking the low road and making vertical dives into a new area of economic activity? Then the project's diversifiability is changing faster. Is the activity spreading horizontally on a high road across many diverse organizations? Then its market intensity is changing faster.

In the first case, the activity favors a few intense *lone wolves*. In the latter case, it favors lots of *dabblers*.

This may matter as you think about what risky ventures you want to undertake. Is your organization better at focus or dabbling? If it's better at focus, prefer projects with lone wolf risks that are unrelated to the overall market. If it's better at dabbling, prefer projects with more market-related risks.

There's a financial difference between lone wolf and dabbler risks that may be even more important. What changes fastest for lone wolf projects is the diversifiability of their risks. But diversifiability is a *debt-holder* concern. In particular, lenders worry whether lack of diversification may impair your ability to pay your debts.

What changes fastest for dabbler projects is the market intensity of their risks. But market intensity is an *equity-holder* concern. It is market-correlated risk that stockholders can't diversify, and they'll need higher returns if they have to bear it.

The risk-role matrix therefore has a financial use for managers looking at companywide risks. It can help them think about how to finance those risks. Risks to the right of the table raise the *market risk* of the whole firm. All things being equal, profit will have to rise, or the stock of the company will fall. Risks at the bottom of the table raise *solvency* concerns. Cash flow must be robust, or the credit rating of the firm will fall.

This means a firm with credit rating concerns may ironically want to favor projects where it can play a customer umbrella or shock absorber role (top). The diversification that lets it absorb risks from business partners gives it a stronger credit rating from the perspective of debt holders or lenders. A firm with stock price concerns may prefer projects where it can play a customer umbrella or classic borrower role (left). It will want to stick to risks that its stockholders can diversify.

In sum, the relative sensitivity to risk of your firm's shareholders and debt holders affects the kinds of projects you may want to pursue. If your credit rating is shaky, you don't want a lot of classic borrower projects, for example. And if your share price is volatile, you don't want to be a shock absorber in lots of sectors.

But the most important thing about risk roles is that even when it comes to random risks, where no one has an advantage in narrowing the uncertainty, you can still create an advantage by choosing your partners carefully. And that choice depends on the nature of the risk. Are you heavily exposed to an idiosyncratic risk? Find diversified partners who can help bear it. Can you diversify a risk with high market intensity? Find partners who will compensate you for absorbing it.

FLAT-FIELD RISKS AND HOW RANDOMNESS CHANGES COMPETITION

The framework of risk networks and risk-role matrices broadens the concept of risk intelligence beyond our own information flows to the information flowing through whole networks of partners. That's why it has something to say about truly random as well as learnable risks. This is a good thing, because the global challenges and opportunities confronting even smaller companies around the world are forcing more and more of us to make choices between learnable and random risks.

So let's take a deep dive on what this broader risk intelligence framework can tell us about the impact of randomness as well as learning speed on our increasingly global search for growth. To start, it's worth highlighting what is most important in the definition of randomness for thinking about business and strategic competition.

As we're using the terms, no one can *assess* truly random risks better than anyone else. This is because no one can reliably predict outcomes with indeterminate causes. Some may be able to *manage* random risks better, but they won't enjoy any structural advantage based on consistently superior predictions.

For example, history may tell me that the worst-case loss I will suffer from refinancing my thirty-year mortgage this month rather than next month is, say, 0.4 percent per year.[3] But it also shows that I have almost no hope of outguessing the market over time: interest rate movements appear to be random. They reflect every bit of information known in a market of thousands of bond traders around the world. So I'm not the only one who hasn't got a clue whether rates will go up or down this month. In fact, nobody knows any more about these rates than I do.

The business implications of true randomness are clearer if we relabel these kinds of uncertainties as *flat-field* risks—risks that present a flat or level playing field where everyone is equally uncertain about them and no one has an advantage in assessing them. Of course, recognizing that a risk is truly random doesn't make the risk go away. But it's often crucially important to know that no one can routinely assess a risk's magnitude or trend line better than you.

Other examples of flat-field risks we have discussed include foreign exchange rates, widely traded commodity prices, stock prices, and indexes of widely traded securities, like the S&P 500. The prices of derivatives based on widely traded bond, commodity, and stock prices and volatilities also seem to move truly randomly.

Plenty of other values are hard to predict, like the weather and the level of a country's economic activity. But they are hard to predict because they have so many complex causes. What distinguishes flat-field risks is that markets come to rest where the forces on a price are in balance. If we could predict what more we might know about those forces at some point in the future, then that itself is information the market should reflect today. Flat-field risks—the risks in prices determined by competitive markets—really are different because they are radically unpredictable.

Most people assume that if surprises, or *unpredicted* risks, are trouble, then truly random, or *unpredictable,* risks must be worse. An advantage of the term *flat-field risks* is that it makes us question this assumption. Flat-field risks surely aren't good news. But might we sometimes prefer them to learnable ones?

ARE FLAT-FIELD RISKS GOOD NEWS OR BAD?

Chapter 2 suggested flat-field risks are not always worse news than learnable ones. It's probably more accurate to say that the randomness of the risks underlying a proposal for a project or an initiative can be seriously *liberating.*

What's liberating about flat-field risks is not the frequency, severity, or inscrutability of the risk. Flat-field and learnable risks can be equally frequent or severe. They can both be perplexing to manage. But learnable risks pose a challenge that flat-field risks do not. There is always the danger that someone else will be in a better position to assess a learnable risk. This can give rise to a sustainable competitive advantage in activities bearing the risk.

There is, on the other hand, no possibility that someone else will be in a better position to assess a flat-field risk. If, for example, we want to launch an investment business driven by rising stock market prices, which move randomly, there's no danger that some competitor will surprise us with more insight into when stock prices rise. (Think of Malkiel's random walks.) However difficult a flat-field risk may be to manage, and however attractive or unattractive the returns on an activity that gives rise to it, there is little danger of *always* knowing less about it than someone else. With flat-field risks, we are all equally in the dark.

When it comes time to judge investments in projects subject to flat-field risks, therefore, one issue is off the table. There are plenty of other reasons to avoid projects and initiatives subject to flat-field risks, such as the possibility that they outweigh the likely rewards. But the danger of systematically under- or overestimating such risks is not a reason. Ignorance, in the case of flat-field risks, is no excuse.

This seems to be especially important in thinking about international opportunities. Suppose, for example, that a senior management team is evaluating a proposal from the general manager of one of its lines of business. The proposal involves building new capacity in an emerging market. And let's say that the senior management team has raised questions for several weeks about all the major risks specific to the project—learnable risks reflecting political, supplier, labor, customer, operational, reputational, and a host of other uncertainties.

At length, the senior management team satisfies itself that with regard to these risks, the potential gains are worth the uncertainties. Furthermore, the senior management team satisfies itself that a better-informed competitor is not likely to blindside the firm with regard to these risks. But still they deny the project.

"We cannot take the risk," they might say, "that someone else will have a better grasp of the commodity prices driving the cost of the new operation. Hence, we have to forgo the opportunity." In other words, the senior management team has fully alerted itself to the growing competitive dimension of risk assessment. But they have misapplied it.

There is no danger in this situation that someone else will have a better grasp of a flat-field risk like the price of competitively traded commodity metal. Once you are satisfied with regard to the level of learnable risks that you face in a project, with regard to your risk intelligence regarding those learnable risks, and with regard to the level of flat-field risks you face in the project, you're done. There's no risk intelligence question concerning a flat-field risk, unless perhaps you're thinking more broadly of networks.

So there really is a sense in which flat-field risks are good news. Provided that the potential profit or gain of an opportunity outweighs your cost of absorbing its associated flat-field risk, you don't need to worry about being best-in-class in assessing it. You can take it.

HOW CREATING A FLAT-FIELD RISK HELPED FREE MEXICO

It helps to look at a real-world example that throws the different challenges posed by learnable and flat-field risks into sharp relief. Our goal should be to develop a sense of how to choose projects subject to a mixed bag of learnable and random risks. This example is useful because it looks at what changes when a *single* risk transforms from one type into another—in this case, from a learnable into a flat-field risk.

In 1986, Senator Bill Bradley (D-NJ), who had hired me as his staff economist, asked me to work up a solution to the debt crisis that was swallowing Mexico. At the time, Mexico's foreign debt was hovering close to $100 billion. The Reagan administration in the United States had tried to paper over the problem by getting banks to make bridge loans to Mexico so Mexico could pay interest on its old debt and avoid a formal default that would hurt the banks. The cash made a round trip from the lender's vaults back to their vaults: the banks showed juicy new loans on their books, and everyone tried to ignore the growing hole in their balance sheets. To make matters worse, the resulting growth in debt caused Mexican investors to take whatever money they could get their hands on and invest it outside their country.

The only way out was to recognize losses on the old loans and start fresh: in other words, instead of more money in, less money out. My job was to build a campaign for "less out" among various interest groups seeking a longer-term solution for Mexico. These included Latin American countries heavily indebted to private banks, U.S. farmers and manufacturers losing big Latin export markets, labor groups that believed foreign indebtedness cost U.S. export jobs, defense folks worried about hemisphere security, religious groups, and the usual foreign aid crowd.

But who wants to recognize loan losses when your borrower might just be crying wolf? What if your borrower really can pay, but feigns distress? The banks had a legitimate reason to fight: they knew very little about the real state of Mexico's economic condition. Debt relief might not be necessary: it could encourage even more profligate borrowing behavior in the future! For the next two years, I compiled evidence that Mexico really needed relief, but had little success convincing the bankers.

Emerging-market specialist Stephen Dizard was convinced there was a business to build around the debt of struggling developing countries. He thought it was possible to make a robust market in these securities. All it required was a clear sense of value.

Like Billy Beane years later in Oakland, Dizard had lots of information at his fingertips. If anyone wanted to trade a bond or even a piece of a loan due from a Mexican borrower, there was a good chance Dizard would hear about it. So why not create an index tracking the market's best sense of the real value of the country's debts? Dizard made it possible to get a more accurate estimate of the current financial landscape of Mexico, without all the obfuscation and dissembling that had taken place in previous years. Within weeks, banks and traders would start the day looking at Dizard's numbers on Mexico, Argentina, and Brazil. People even tracked it in Congress.

The effect was like turning on a light in a dark room. Every corner was illuminated.

No one predicted what happened next. Suddenly, the banks' resistance to debt relief melted away. The Reagan administration was stunned. The banks could now judge Mexico's ability to pay. After that, there was no difference between new loans and debt relief. It was time to take losses. In fact, everyone saw the advantage of debt relief as a means of stopping capital flight.

Dizard's index did nothing to reduce the level of risk in Mexican debt. What it did was reduce the uncertainty around the country's actual ability-to-pay to a flat-field risk. You did not know the absolute truth, but you knew that nobody, not even the head of Mexico's central bank, knew any more than you. And that's precisely when everyone waded in and took on the risk of debt relief. They knew they wouldn't be someone else's sucker. The banks' reduction of their uncertainty to a flat-field risk opened the way to nearly a decade of economic growth in Mexico.

It's not every day that someone turns an ordinary, learnable risk, where everyone should worry about competitive advantage, into a flat-field risk, where no one faces a harder risk assessment challenge than anyone else. It happens pretty much only when someone creates a new financial market. But it's a powerful example of how the world can change when the nature of a major risk changes.

EMERGING-MARKET RISK, FOREIGN DIRECT INVESTMENT, AND BUYERS OF LAST RESORT

As European birthrates and U.S. consumer spending decline, growth becomes harder for companies to achieve. The search for growth is consequentially taking U.S. and European firms in the direction of the new and unfamiliar risks of emerging markets, where birthrates are not so low and spending is poised to take off.

This is more widespread than the recent surge in outsourcing. Outsourcing takes advantage of just one thing: lower cost. Many emerging markets have something to offer of longer consequence, however. Their economies have the potential for enormous growth if they start to close their income and wealth gap with developed countries. And companies facing growth slowdowns in Europe and America can participate in that growth if they can figure out how to handle the risks emerging markets present.

These risks are a mixture of learnable and flat-field risks. Often, the two are inextricably intertwined. A project may, for example, be equally subject to a risky emerging-market exchange rate—a flat-field risk—and its host country's political risks, which are learnable. What lessons on partners apply to these risks?

The traditional approach to managing direct investment risk in emerging markets has been control. Because the risks are poorly understood, management teams have tended to insist on as near-complete operating control as possible. This often involves detailed operating procedures and managers from the investing country. And it usually involves a majority or controlling position in the venture's equity. But operating control is not always best. An understanding of risk roles helps determine when it is.

Operating control does make sense if your strategy is to absorb your local partners' risk. The story of Lao Textiles provides a compelling example.

When Carol Cassidy, an American aid worker and textile expert, went to Laos in 1989, she found the silk weaving craft of the country with one of the richest textile traditions in the world all but dead. Insisting on 100 percent ownership, mastering traditional Lao textile design, and engineering her own looms, Cassidy finally launched a weaving factory in a dry, open concrete outbuilding next to an old French mansion on a dirt road in the Lao capital, Vientiane.

Why was it important for Cassidy to own an enterprise in a Communist country that had no idea what to think of a private company? The risk challenge she faced appears at first to be an exception to the rules of risk roles but really isn't.

Cassidy looked a little like a classic borrower. For one thing, the project's diversifiability was low: as a textile artist and aid worker, she had no other businesses to diversify her Lao exposure. For another, the market intensity of the project's risks was low: the principal risk in restarting a dying traditional textile craft was highly specific to her business.

Cassidy nevertheless needed to act as a shock absorber to get her business off the ground. The problem was that villages had stopped bothering with the labor-intensive process of preparing silk thread as modern synthetics became available and as opium cultivation proved a much more profitable alternative. "It was difficult to find villages that would trust that if they made the silk, I would really buy it," she recalls.[4]

In other words, traditional Lao silk weaving was so flat on its back that even a lone entrepreneuse proposing to sell into competitive western markets was in a better position than local partners to absorb the venture's business risk. And from the perspective of a country largely cut off from the rest of the world since the Indochinese wars, western markets were a mystery. There was no way to know westerners might prefer the spectacular designs of ancient Lao weavers to Mickey Mouse shirts. To a large extent, market uncertainty is what had disrupted the sector, not supply problems. Cassidy brokered this product market risk for local craftspeople and businesses and succeeded.

Her industry now employs two hundred workers, and Cassidy's Lao Textiles has exceedingly low turnover. Her textiles hang in museums around the world.

While Lao Textiles may have looked like a classic borrower, there's a reason Cassidy played the role of shock absorber. Her suppliers had even fewer diversification options than she and needed protection from unfamiliar western markets. In the context of Lao Textile's risk network, what mattered were the needs of Cassidy's potential partners. Operating control made sense since Cassidy would absorb a lot of network risk.

And yet it's not always necessary or even best to assert such operating control. If the natural price of control is bearing a lot of risk, it may be better to distribute control in an emerging-market risk network to get local partners to bear more risk. In fact, distributing control may be essential when local partners understand some of the risks better than you. Neil Gaskell, the former longtime treasurer of Shell Oil and now board member of the London School of Economics, gives a clear example of where transferring some risk and control to a local partner in the form of equity proved crucial.

In a stint running some of Shell's operations in the Sultanate of Brunei on Borneo, Gaskell needed to find a contractor to run the company's fleet of cars. Ford and Toyota owned dealerships in the little kingdom, but their local partners had reputations for inefficiency. An ambitious local businessman, whom we'll call Mr. Ibrahim, proposed to take over the Ford dealership and shoulder the largest risks for three years if he could count on Shell's business.

And Gaskell agreed, but he did not rely on his judgment of character and local knowledge to make the decision. He might have, since he had absorbed a great deal about Borneo during his three-year rotation. He once astonished a knot of Texas oilmen in Washington, D.C., for example, by demonstrating an exotic Dayak bird dance that he had learned in a remote longhouse on a trek through the jungle.

But the key to distributing the operating risks Shell faced in Brunei was not local knowledge or cultural intimacy, as important as they can be. It was making sure Ibrahim could really absorb the considerable risk of keeping a fleet of cars working on the north coast of Borneo. To do so, he would have to be able to reap sizable rewards.

What Gaskell provided, in the end, was more valuable than capital. He committed Shell as a *stable customer* and enabled Ibrahim to build up an independent business. With the prospect of a viable dealership, Ibrahim could find the risk capital.

Ibrahim's business served Shell well. Moreover, it became one of the most successful car dealerships in the Brunei capital city. Gaskell thinks it was the prospect of that broader success that ensured the dealer could serve Shell reliably as it started up.

To some extent, Gaskell was in the position of a classic borrower: he couldn't diversify fleet operating risk from unreliable providers. And there was little in the way of contract enforcement in Brunei to serve as insurance. The lesson seems to be that if you must play the role of classic borrower, but there are no third parties around who can bear or reduce risk, look to see whether your suppliers can absorb it. But you must make sure they have the capacity and incentive to do so. For classic borrowers in unfamiliar markets, relinquishing control can be more effective than tightening it.

Part of the lesson in risk partnership is to build supplier communities so the people nearest a remote project have as strong an interest in seeing it thrive as you do. Cassidy did this by opening a new market to Lao weavers. Gaskell did this by making sure his partner could attract risk capital. In general, the broader the network of local suppliers you build, the stronger will be your constituency for solving political problems. Even if a local supply chain is more expensive than your home market suppliers, it may pay for itself by absorbing local risks you are not in a position to manage.

The active involvement with local suppliers that risk roles imply may be of central importance to development, too. For example, it's obvious that hiring a local supplier for your Peruvian sneaker factory is better for Peru than hiring a supplier from Cleveland. But what's not obvious is that hiring local suppliers may be more important than the cash that direct investment injects into the developing economy.

Few foreign firms act as "lenders of last resort" in successful emerging-market development stories. They don't have to. Poor countries are often awash with savings. But foreign direct investors often seem to play the role of "buyer of last resort." And their greatest impact often seems to be indirect.

Once Gaskell contracted with Ibrahim in Borneo, for example, a virtuous cycle ensued. Gaskell had broken new ground. He hadn't struck a deal with someone just because everybody else had. He hadn't struck a deal with a friend of his brother-in-law or a politician's buddy. He had struck a deal on the merits.

Ibrahim, in turn, needed subcontractors. He would do the same thing. The whole supply chain would start to become competitive. Open and competitive contracting on a fair basis will crowd out backroom deals once it gets started. This may be the greatest value investors create.

The role of direct investors in rationalizing contracting and hiring procedures suggests something larger. It suggests that demand may in some ways be as important as supply in determining development outcomes. More rational procurement may send clearer signals to producers about how to create wealth. And buyers of last resort may be critical for boosting growth by helping to rationalize demand.

THE OPEN MARKET AND ITS ENEMIES

Whether we want to improve our own risk intelligence or the performance of our risk networks, our customers play a critical role. They are our most important source of risk intelligence in the sense of commercial feedback. And they are central players in our risk networks. One of the greatest benefits of the concept of risk intelligence is the light it throws on what makes a great customer.

Of course, customers can't reduce the level of a risk. But they can share it. A loyal customer who has trusted your innovations in the past may be all it takes to make you an extraordinarily successful innovator. The question is whether there are customer attributes beyond loyalty that can be a source of advantage in handling risk.

The answer comes from the fundamental role of customers in an economy. Customers are the ultimate critics in a market. We can think of them as providing the natural habitat in which businesses and even governments compete. Entrepreneurs and managers who adapt well to the demands of customers prosper; others die out. Customers set the direction in which managers and entrepreneurs need to try to go.

When we say it's a hard world out there, we often mean the economy is full of challenges. But the reason is that it's unclear what we need to do to thrive or even survive in it. Our risk intelligence is what helps us survive under such uncertainty. So part of risk intelligence should be finding the microenvironments that will either insulate us from the rude surprises of the wider market or strengthen us to deal with them. Part of risk intelligence is finding customers who make us stronger.

As businesspeople, at one level, we all know this. We talk about "customer loyalty" that can guarantee steady business in downturns and in the face of brash competitors offering deals too good to be true. We seek out loyalty and try to understand what drives it so we can nurture and even promote it.

We also talk about "strategic customers" who teach us to be great salespeople, marketers, manufacturers, designers, technologists, organizers, or communicators. We seek them out, serve them well, and try to retain them.

What we don't often do is generalize this idea. We don't often ask which *markets* will be best for us. Instead, we tend to focus on whichever customers we think will be most loyal or strategic, and chase them. Odds are that most other firms and organizations in our line of work are after the same people. This leads to the modern American phenomenon of saturation-bombing certain zip codes with print catalogues.

Let's take a closer look at how to generalize the idea of an attractive customer. What makes a market especially effective in strengthening our enterprises and honing our own skills? Why might one regional or demographically defined market make the people and organizations that serve it more durable even outside of it?

Since the essence of a market is the customers who constitute it, and customers are basically the final critics of their providers, we're really asking what drives the critical capability of a market. We're asking what drives the value of a market's feedback.

But this is right where we started. When we began to measure risk intelligence, we asked what made one person's or organization's information better than another's for assessing a new risk. We answered that question. Among other things, it's the surprise and relevance of that information. If we want to score the value of the feedback we'll get from different markets, we should start with the same two concepts.

To take a specific example, imagine you've decided to sell life insurance and retirement products for an agency in town. The agency gives you a choice of two geographically defined districts. Suppose you have two goals: finding a district that will give you a good start in the business but also one that will get you ready for anything. How can you apply risk intelligence concepts to choosing the best available district?

Of course, it will depend largely on how well they're already served. But suppose one position has opened in each of two districts, and you think the business opportunities are roughly equal. In that case, it's natural to ask which district has more of the features that characterize heavy insurance buyers. In a steady-state market, though, you can assume that past agents have done their best. Ready buyers have already attracted the most attention. So there's no telling what will make for the next great opportunity.

In that case, you'll focus on what you can learn from the two districts. Start with the surprise of the feedback you can expect to get from calling on each district. You flip back two chapters and recall that what makes an experience surprising is its improbability. But that's not directly transferable to choosing a district. After all, we don't want to end up in the district with the most improbable sales!

But improbability is nevertheless the right idea. The most probable result from a series of sales calls is a set of weak and inconsistent customer responses. Strong and consistent responses—that is to say, coherent responses—are less probable, and if they're positive, they really suggest we're on the right track. If you're going to learn to be a great salesperson, you want to start off in a market where best practices are sharply defined, and you need coherent responses to define them.

Coherent responses depend in part on customer sensitivity to product and service variations. If your customers are too hard-pressed, distracted, or uninterested in what you sell to pay attention to improvements, you won't get a clear readout on their value.

Coherence also depends on the consistency of customer responses. Market segments can come later. In the beginning, you want all your prospects pushing in the same direction.

In other words, you want the district with the most integrated market. And you want to avoid the district with the most fragmented market. An integrated market sends consistently reinforced signals to any seller. A fragmented market may create a lot of niche opportunities, but any broader signals will be diluted and confused.

Market integration is the sort of thing we know when we see it. Measuring it is another matter altogether. But the most general approach is to gauge what economists call the *concavity* of what a market values. Suppose your customers are ambivalent about two combinations of features or services. You would say their preferences are concave if they preferred any combination of the packages to either of the packages. (If you tried to picture this on a graph for just two features, the ambivalence lines would be concave.)

If you don't happen to have a handy concavity index for your agency's sales districts, trust your instincts. Which district seems most homogeneous and unified? Which has the fewest internal divisions? Which has the least disparity in income?

Let's move on to the other of the two core factors in the risk intelligence score. What is the relevance of the feedback you will get from calling on each district? You always have to define relevance with respect to a specific problem. (More precisely, you have to define it with respect to the possible answers to the problem you're considering.) To what problem does the relevance of feedback from a sales district matter?

It must be learning to sell into the typical district in the rest of the country. So which district will provide the feedback most relevant to honing insurance sales skills we can carry almost anywhere? Presumably, it will be the district that most resembles the national market. At a minimum, we'll probably want to match the range and average of demographics like income and age for the larger market.

Suppose one of the two local districts really does resemble the whole country. But it's fragmented, just like the country as a whole. And let's say that the other district is homogeneous but fails to reflect the diversity of the country as a whole. The trouble is that coherence is pulling us in one direction, and relevance is pulling us in the other.

Unfortunately, this is the way the world really is. Let's call the local markets like the insurance districts in this example *incubator markets.* Then experience suggests most incubator markets fail the coherence test (sensitivity and integration) or the relevance test (representativeness). It's one of the reasons that overcoming the risks surrounding a new venture is so hard. But it leads to a surprisingly strong lesson about the nature of the larger national markets that host the world's innovators, managers, and entrepreneurs.

The conclusion is that national markets that are fragmented or marked by large disparities in income will develop more slowly than others, all other things being equal. The reason is that corporate ventures, start-up companies, and other innovative projects will not be able to find effective incubator markets within them.

These ventures may indeed find incubator markets that are representative of their fragmented national markets. But the markets will lack the coherence—the strength and consistency of customer responses—to be found in successful incubator markets, like the example of the highly integrated district sketched earlier. In fact, every incubator market within a fragmented national market will fail to be either coherent or representative.

This makes intuitive sense. It's easy to imagine how even a small start-up in China can hope to grow. Suppose it starts in a small coastal town marked by the consistency of the preferences of its local consumers. The town will provide feedback that's highly coherent. But once the start-up figures out how to serve the town, it will be in a good position to expand to the extent the town is representative of China's national—or at least coastal—market. So the integration of the larger Chinese market should accelerate growth.

At the same time, it's harder to imagine how start-ups manage to grow in India. The talent pouring out of its top schools is overwhelming. But what local market in India reflects the diversity of the whole country? What town captures even the basic mix of India's Aryan culture in the north and Dravidian culture in the south? And if such an incubator market did exist, how on earth would start-ups sort out the signals it sent? The fragmentation of India's national market weakens the effectiveness of potential incubator markets. This is a development problem independent of corruption.

In perhaps the most remarkable chapter of his remarkable survey of development economics, *The Elusive Quest for Growth,* William Easterly neglects to emphasize that much of the gripping work on "polarized peoples" is his own.[5] He writes:

> *The worst case for good policymaking and political freedom is to have both high inequality and high ethnic diversity . . . Development failures like Chiapas, Guatemala, Sierra Leone, and Zambia are examples of the fatal mixture of ethnic and class hatreds. In contrast, development successes like Denmark, Japan, and South Korea . . . have benefited from high social consensus associated with low inequality and ethnic homogeneity.[6]*

In fact, he provides data showing that countries polarized by both race and class, like Bolivia, Guatemala, and Zambia, all have low economic growth.[7] He explains it with incentives, one of the major themes of his book. If ethnically distinct groups coexist at radically different levels of income in a country, the incentive for the poorer group to claw back wealth from the richer group may outweigh any other incentives to make money. The coincidence of ethnic distinctions and wide income disparities looks like a "poisonous cocktail" from an economic development perspective.

The concept of risk ecologies suggests an impact of market fragmentation that may be even more systematic than the dysfunctional incentives Easterly has described. Market fragmentation may block the path of individual projects and enterprises to growth by ruling out microenvironments that can be simultaneously coherent and representative.

Take in turn the poisons of income disparity and ethnic fragmentation Easterly identified as enemies of the open market. Income disparity, in an incubator market, is likely to mix up positive and negative signals from customers and muddy the lessons innovators and managers can learn from them. But if the larger economy has high inequality, only incubator markets with large disparities of income will be representative of it. One of the tragic ironies of the developing world is that so many poor countries have the high income disparities that make representative local incubator markets rare.

Ethnic fragmentation is the other enemy of the open market. For a local incubator market to mimic or represent the national market of Iraq, for example, it would have to include Shia, Sunnis, and Kurds. There are neighborhoods with that diversity in Baghdad. But they would make very poor incubator markets because their conflicting traditional preferences would (and do) provide highly confusing feedback to fledgling businesses.

Fragmentation on this view appears to be an enemy of the open markets that enterprises need to grow. It reflects a failure in the delivery of effective feedback or criticism to producers and providers about what creates value. And without that feedback, producers and providers can neither raise their risk intelligence nor build effective risk networks. But that doesn't mean fragmentation is bad in itself. It just means it may hamper development.

In *The Open Society and Its Enemies,* Karl Popper argues that we should seek openness in society to secure freedom from tyranny.[8] And we should promote free and robust criticism to ensure that openness. Successful personal and economic growth similarly requires effective criticism. Criticism weeds out unpromising economic activity just the way a local ecology discourages poor species adaptations. But the openness needed to promote productive economic criticism in a market does not necessarily coincide with the openness a society needs to protect itself from arbitrary authority.

Cultural diversity can *promote* the critical exchange of views and reinforce the openness of society. And yet it may *inhibit* economic development. Mali, for example, is a democratic success but a development tragedy. It has dozens of languages, including representatives of four unrelated language families: Niger-Congo, Nilo-Saharan, Afro-Asiatic, and Indo-European. It is stupendously diverse. But that diversity may well be keeping its economic growth desperately slow.

Emerging markets may in some cases face a trade-off between factors promoting openness in their society and those promoting openness in their markets. The policy solution is always to try to overcome those trade-offs. But it is irresponsible to pretend they are not there. Parts of the world are poor because elites support corruption. Others are poor because they really lack viable opportunities. We must distinguish between the two.

This theory of the ramifications of risk ecologies and the importance of market integration has immediate implications for Europe. Many commentators argue that the European Union's market integration efforts have bogged down. They point to the particularly poor records of France and Italy in implementing market-opening measures. But integration may be essential for Europe ever to match the economic performance of the United States. And matching that performance will only grow in importance as Europe goes through a significant demographic transition to an older society in coming years.

But if on this view the lack of integration is a problem for Europe, income disparities may be one for the United States. The well-documented growth in U.S. income disparity appears to be a very bad sign for the country's long-term prospects. As a permanent upper class starts to establish itself in American society, it will grow harder and harder for individuals and groups to find local markets representative of the country's income differentials. But only non-representative incubator markets will have the coherence in income levels needed for clear feedback on the economic value of new ideas. So we could start to lose what may have propelled American prosperity in the twentieth century: a homogeneous national market.

An even greater irony is that the vast, integrated middle-class market of America has probably served as an excellent surrogate to guide and develop emerging export-oriented economies like China, South Korea, and Brazil. If income disparity starts to close the U.S. market, though, this chapter of global economic development must end.

6

Raising Your Risk Intelligence Systematically

Our risk intelligence directly affects the success of our plans and strategies. But the fit between our goals and risk skills is also a product of those plans and strategies. It's a major consequence of what we decide to do with our time and resources, or where and how we try to compete. Since our choices affect our risk intelligence and it affects our success with those choices, it becomes a central concern in making decisions.

The story starts with an abstract question: how learnable and random risks differ. It continues with a way to measure our risk intelligence based on the complementary ideas of surprise and relevance drawn from probability and information theory. Those measurements let us add risk strategy audits to our planning toolkits. And the story ends with a look at the partnership implications of risk ecologies. In other words, the story runs the gamut of metaphysics, applied mathematics, the economics of the firm, and corporate finance.

Here are ten steps that distil the implications of the story of risk intelligence. They start with things to do tomorrow and end with ways of rethinking our businesses and economy. I've grouped the steps under the rules of risk intelligence that they flesh out, which are shown in bold.

Recognize which risks are learnable.

Identify risks you can learn about fastest.

Sequence risky projects in a "learning pipeline."

Keep networks of partners to manage all risks.

STEP 1: CHOOSE PROJECTS, PROBLEMS, AND VENTURES WITH LEARNABLE RISKS IN MIND

One of the most basic decisions every one of us must make is how to spend our time and allocate our resources. We define goals. We construct alternatives. We project results. Then we choose the alternative with the best result. Or do we?

The problem is the quality of the projections. Some will be better than average, and some will be worse. But what if we are worse than average at projecting results from our best alternatives? For example, suppose we work for an insurance company and we think business credit is the best new line of business. If we have a poor handle on credit risk, we could be headed for serious trouble.

This problem does not arise with the market risks banks have managed for a hundred years because market risks are random, and no bank has an enduring advantage in assessing them. What's new regarding learnable risks is that we're beginning to record their effects in our lives and businesses. And that's why differences in the quality of our projections are becoming apparent and starting to matter.

We're basically watching a new competitive front open up. We know our companies compete on direct costs like capital equipment and labor productivity. And we know they compete on customer management and market segmentation. Now they are competing on risk-based advantages like risk intelligence. And it affects everyone with responsibility for a P&L, a division, resources, sales goals, or project management.

So a critical new step in choosing how to spend your time or allocate your resources emerges. You need to ask which of your risks are learnable. For many initiatives, there will be a mix. But for a first approximation, you should separate projects that you're considering that bear market risks from projects with other risks that may be learnable. And you should ask whether you have an advantage in learning about the latter.

Recognize which risks are learnable.

Identify risks you can learn about fastest.

Sequence risky projects in a "learning pipeline."

Keep networks of partners to manage all risks.

STEP 2: SCORE YOUR RISK INTELLIGENCE FOR THE OPTIONS YOU'RE CONSIDERING AND TRIAGE THEM

For each major risk of each major project, problem, decision, or initiative you're considering, score your risk intelligence. Give yourself a 0, 1, or 2 for each of the score's five factors for each risk (see table 6-1). Give yourself a 2 if you think you're able to assess the risk and its changing causes better than others facing it. Give yourself a 1 if you're average, and a 0 if you may be weaker. Scores fall between 0 and 10; 5 is average.

Now rank the projects by your risk intelligence scores. You should ask yourself some hard questions about pursuing the projects with the weakest scores. And you may want to allocate more resources to the ones where you expect to learn fastest.

TABLE 6-1

Risk intelligence score

How often do you have experiences related to the risk?	
How relevant are these experiences to what might influence the risk?	
How surprising are these experiences?	
How diverse are these experiences as sources of information?	
How methodically do you keep track of what you learn from them?	
Total	

STEP 3: LOOK FOR PATTERNS IN YOUR RISK INTELLIGENCE SCORES AND TRY TO IMPROVE THEM

Check to see whether there are patterns in your scores. In particular, see whether you or your organization fits the pattern of an impressionist, encyclopedist, or amnesiac (see table 6-2).

The *impressionist* is decisive, perhaps too decisive, and draws from a number of surprising experiences that have had a formative effect on her. But she may apply those experiences where they are not really relevant. A remedy is wider experience.

The *encyclopedist* has a smattering of knowledge pertinent to many of an organization's activities. But they tend not to be surprising or "hard won" and as a consequence give him a weak basis for decisions. A remedy is more intense experience, typically in customer-facing roles.

The *amnesiac* enjoys a good store of memorable experiences relevant to an organization's current problems. But she tends to have trouble prioritizing and communicating those experiences to colleagues. The best remedy is for colleagues to find productive ways to debrief her over time.

More generally, managers should assess the risk intelligence types of their teams. Teams well balanced across the strengths of the impressionist, encyclopedist, and amnesiac can be formidable.

TABLE 6-2

Which type of learner are you?

	Impressionists	Encyclopedists	Amnesiacs
Amount of experience	1	1	2
Relevance of experience	0	2	1
Surprise of experience	2	0	1
Diversity of experiences	1	1	1
Record keeping	1	1	0
Total	5	5	5

Recognize which risks are learnable.

Identify risks you can learn about fastest.

Sequence risky projects in a "learning pipeline."

Keep networks of partners to manage all risks.

STEP 4: CONDUCT A RISK STRATEGY
AUDIT FOR YOUR MAIN ACTIVITIES

Audit your risk strategy. And you didn't think you had one! But of
course you do, and it's determined by the way you (or your organization) spend your time and resources. For a company, it's as simple as
the major risks in its lines of business. For a sales manager, it could
be the territories of the sales force or product groups. For an IT or
operations manager, it could be major projects or process improvements. For just about all of us, it could be alternative ways of meeting
our performance goals for the year.

What matters to a risk strategy? This book argues, of course, that
your risk intelligence for each major risk is crucial. But the other
critical factor is how much each of your major risks diversifies

the rest of your risks. So for each risk, you want to capture your relative skill in assessing it and the extent to which it diversifies your net risk.

A graph that captures this information might look like the one in figure 6-1. Each circle represents the major risk of a different activity, project, or division. Circle size usually reflects a project's contribution to your income or your firm's revenue. But it could also reflect how much time you spend on it.

The graph captures the risk intelligence score for each risk along the horizontal axis, and it captures the diversifiability of each risk along the vertical. So risks that you assess well and that your other risks diversify appear in the upper right, those that you assess well but that your other risks cannot diversify appear in the lower right, and so forth.

Risks tend to start at the upper left because we usually aren't good at assessing them at first, and they are easily diversified since the projects they underlie are small. As we get better at understanding a risk, it moves to the right. As the project it underlies grows, our other risks cannot diversify it as well, and it moves down. If we decide to stop monitoring the factors driving the risk, it moves left. So the risks underlying our projects tend to migrate clockwise from upper left to lower left. They form a curving pipeline.

FIGURE 6-1

Risk strategy audit tool: portfolio view

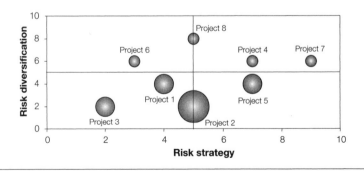

A major use of the graph is to identify holes and clumps in the pipeline. Clumps signal a need to learn too much at once. Holes signal a missed opportunity to put our learning resources to work that we may regret if our main activities lose their luster.

STEP 5: CLASSIFY YOUR NEW RISK PIPELINE IN TERMS OF GAPS THAT THREATEN GROWTH

If you run a P&L, compare your risk strategy with your growth strategy (see figure 6-2). A traditional way to picture a growth strategy is to picture each business activity in terms of the growth of its market and the company's competitive position or share of that market. Once again, each business activity appears as a circle whose size may represent revenue.

The results of a risk strategy audit and a matrix for the growth and share of the markets of a set of business activities share many features. The verticals—diversification of risk and market growth—capture features of the business activities. The horizontals—risk intelligence and, usually, market share—capture the company's position in those businesses. Most importantly, business activities tend to migrate clockwise in both.

This last feature lets you inspect visually whether a given project's or activity's growth profile is "aging" faster than its risk profile. This

FIGURE 6-2

Risk strategy matrix versus growth strategy matrix

FIGURE 6-3

Four seasons of risk strategy patterns

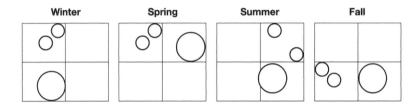

would be the situation where the circle for that activity had moved farther clockwise on the matrix for its growth strategy than on the matrix for its risk strategy. That might argue for an early exit from the business before risk problems overwhelm its early profitability.

You should also characterize the strengths and weaknesses of your overall risk strategy. Are there enough experiments? Have you developed enough pockets of expertise? Are the risks overconcentrated? Or are you dividing your time among too many learning challenges? Figure 6-3 shows four patterns that can help.

For each of these matrices, once again, the vertical reflects diversification, and the horizontal reflects risk intelligence. Winter strategies are risk strategies with little dominance. Spring strategies have little focus. Summer strategies lack development. And fall strategies lack resilience.

These patterns can help explain performance surprises and may suggest remedies that better "fill" a risk pipeline. But they also simplify questions of strategic "fit" between potential individual or corporate partners. And they tell a lot about the attractiveness of potential acquisition candidates a company may want to buy.

Recognize which risks are learnable.

Identify risks you can learn about fastest.

Sequence risky projects in a "learning pipeline."

Keep networks of partners to manage all risks.

STEP 6: COMPARE THE RISK-ROLE MATRIX FOR YOUR ACTIVITIES WITH YOUR RISK PARTNER NETWORKS

Whether you run a division, manage a project list, or control resources, you should think about the network of potential risk-sharing partners in which you work. The nature of the risks you face determines what roles you should play in that network.

Risk roles depend on our random, or *flat-field,* risks as well as our learnable risks. With flat-field risks, there is no danger that someone else will systematically outperform you on the strength of superior risk assessment. And there is no danger that they will use that knowledge to price you out of a market. But your success with both kinds of risk depends on how you distribute the burden they impose across the network of suppliers, partners, and customers who are exposed to them along with you.

To think about the roles different members of a network can play in absorbing or distributing risks, you can plot your major risks on a risk-role matrix (see figure 6-4). As in matrices for risk strategy audits, the major risk for each project or business activity would appear as a circle. Circle size would correspond to revenue or time spent on the project. And as in matrices for risk strategy audits, the matrix's vertical captures the diversifiability of each risk.

FIGURE 6-4

Risk-role matrix

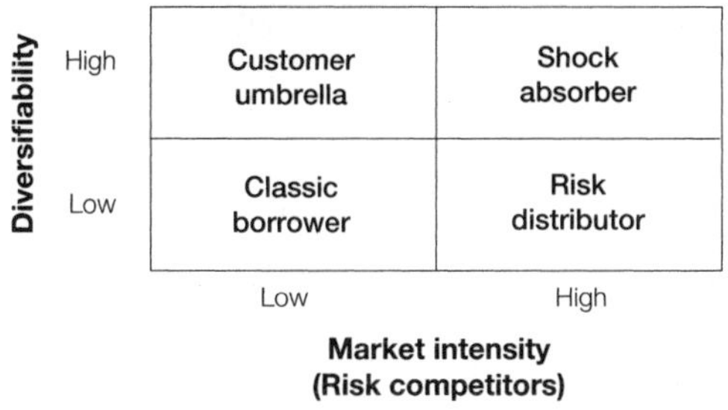

		Low	High
Diversifiability	High	Customer umbrella	Shock absorber
	Low	Classic borrower	Risk distributor

Market intensity
(Risk competitors)

What's different is the horizontal of a risk-role matrix. It captures the *market intensity* of each risk. Think of it as the portion of the variability in results due to risk that correlates with the stock market. (A precise measure would be the so-called Sharpe ratio of the risk, which divides market-driven returns by total risk. Higher Sharpe ratios correspond to higher market intensities.)

The matrix gives the ideal role you can play in handling the risk represented by each circle you plot for one of your projects or business activities. For example, you will want to play the role of customer umbrella for low–market intensity risks that you can diversify. Since you can diversify the risk, it makes sense to absorb it from your suppliers and customers if they will compensate you to do so. And since the risk has low market intensity, it more likely reflects uncertainties in supply than in demand. So it is your customers who will usually be in the weakest position to evaluate this kind of risk.

With low–market intensity risks that you cannot diversify, you will find yourself in the position of the classic borrower. Banks and other investors should be particularly willing to help shoulder the risk because its low market intensity means it has low market correlation. Even if you cannot diversify it, they can.

For risks with high market intensity that you can diversify, you may want to play the role of shock absorber. Once again, your ability to diversify the risk puts you in a good position to absorb it from customers and suppliers willing to compensate you for doing so. But now the high market intensity of the risk means it has a large market component. All other things being equal, that suggests the main uncertainty may lie in market demand. And if that's the case, it is your suppliers who will have the least visibility into the risk and may need the most protection from it.

That leaves the class of risks with high market intensity that you cannot diversify. These are tough. Their high market intensity implies a high market correlation that could prevent financial intermediaries from diversifying them. But you may still want help in bearing these risks. To the extent their high market intensity arises from customer uncertainty, you probably won't be able to get customers to "take back" the risks their behavior creates. So you will have to turn to your suppliers for help, and your role becomes that of a risk distributor.

STEP 7: COMPARE THE RISK ROLES THAT FIT YOUR ORGANIZATION WITH WHAT FITS YOUR RISKS

Risks tend to follow one of two paths across a risk-role matrix. Risks following the "low road" underlie activities suited to a few "lone wolf" organizations and only gradually become more widespread in the economy. For example, craft beers in the United States attracted only specialists until the 1990s, when they became much more widespread. As these activities grow more important to the organizations focusing on them, their risks drop on a risk-role matrix. They move from left to right only later when rising marketwide interest in them increases their market intensity. They reflect discontinuous change (see figure 6-5).

Just the reverse is true of "high road" risks. They underlie initiatives or activities that many "dabbler" organizations take up without focusing on them. Over time, a few specialists may emerge, but only after the underlying risks have grown fairly widespread. For example, most companies have preferred to build their own Web sites rather than rely on specialists to host them. These risks correspond to more continuous innovation.

FIGURE 6-5

Low-road and high-road risk-role migration paths

With a risk-role matrix for your principal risks in front of you, ask these questions. Are more of your risks low-road or high-road risks? And are you, or is your organization, more of a lone wolf or a dabbler?

If you are more effective at lone wolf projects requiring a lot of focus, you should probably concentrate on low-road risks. These are typically activities requiring a focus that large, diversified firms cannot provide. They also require a good credit rating.

If your organization is more effective at dabbling in many experiments, it should probably pursue more risks that follow a high-road trajectory. These activities tend to suit organizations that can diversify and thus absorb high-road risks. Since such risks tend, by definition, to grow market-correlated quickly, your organization's ability to diversify them will be especially valuable. They could nevertheless add to the price pressure on stocks already subject to a lot of market risk.

STEP 8: LOOK FOR OPPORTUNITIES TO TRANSFORM LEARNABLE RISKS INTO FLAT-FIELD RISKS

As a longer-term step, if you have P&L, sales or procurement responsibilities, you may want to mitigate the competitive danger that you may fall behind in assessing the learnable risks you face. List your principal learnable risks and your risk intelligence scores for them. For those you have to bear despite low scores, ask yourself whether anything could transform them into flat-field risks.

Suppose you are exposed to a lot of risk around the residual value of equipment you must eventually resell. And suppose you feel you have no special advantage in assessing that risk. If so, you may be able to change the nature of the risk itself.

For example, you may be able to promote the development of a market in the equipment. Of course, these opportunities are rare. It's harder than just putting old equipment or furniture on eBay. But it may be possible to create a template for capturing whatever drives the equipment's resale value. And it may be possible to identify a community of buyers and sellers who would all prefer transparent pricing.

If so, the effect of the market's pricing on the risk you bear in the resale value of residual equipment will change it. It will transform from a learnable into a flat-field risk. You will no longer be at a disadvantage to others who might have a better grasp of the value of the equipment. And your low risk intelligence score will no longer matter.

STEP 9: CHECK WHETHER YOUR LAUNCH MARKET FOR AN IDEA IS RELEVANT TO YOUR TARGET MARKET

Customers are one of the main sources of intelligence about most of the learnable risks that innovators and entrepreneurs face. For one thing, they tell us what may help or hinder doing more business with them. But when a start-up or a corporate venture is small, the intelligence our initial customers provide may be more important for what it tells us about the larger market we hope to serve.

One of the questions the risk intelligence score asks you about feedback from your customers is its relevance. Does it help you determine what really drives the larger risks you face? If those larger risks have to do with your prospects in a larger market, then the question is really about the relevance of your initial customer feedback to that market. In other words, our earliest and best customers train us. But do they train us to meet the big challenges we want to address, like cracking a national market?

It helps if our "starter" market is like the nationwide and even global markets many companies try to serve. But that often requires a degree of homogeneity and integration in our national markets that just doesn't exist. For example, you may write or sell some software for tracking progress in large projects that is popular with government contractors in Washington, D.C. But it may not sell outside the government sector.

In a case like this, you may have to force yourself to serve customers you don't understand. In fact, there is a risk if you don't. There is a risk you will never train yourself to serve the larger market. And the risk that you won't break out of your starter market is greater if that market is just large enough to keep you going.

So this step runs counter to the venerable wisdom of Marshall Field and John Wanamaker that the customer is always right. The customer may be right about herself. But she may not be right about the larger market we want to understand. The intelligence she provides to us may not be relevant to the risks we want to tackle.

This step is hard because every sales force targets the customers most likely to accept a product. But when we're starting out, we must also target customers who don't particularly like what we offer. We must also seek customers who will open our eyes to the needs we aren't fulfilling but might. We must learn as well as sell.

STEP 10: LOOK FOR OPPORTUNITIES TO BREAK THE COMPROMISE BETWEEN RISK AND GROWTH

Strategists, finance executives, and business leaders constantly wrestle with what looks like a hard trade-off between growth and risk. Many of the companies whose risk and growth strategies we've compared seem better at one than the other. High-growth companies take risks they haven't mastered. And high–risk intelligence companies poke along in low-growth sectors. Growth and risk often feel like a compromise that's hard to break. Growth comes at the expense of risk. Low risk comes at the expense of growth.

But nothing in a risk intelligence score dictates this. I don't mean to aggrandize what a risk intelligence score can tell us about life in general. But it tells us a lot about how information bears on risk. And there is no reason high growth should force low scores on risk intelligence factors for the amount, relevance, surprise, diversity, or records of our business experience. In fact, high growth should improve some of those factors. So, high growth need not impair risk intelligence.

It's easier to see why high–risk intelligence players may feel trapped in low-growth businesses. At some bright point in the future, for example, the best heart valve maker in the world may run out of hearts in its home market that require its product. But just to write this example, I had to add *in its home market.* It will be a very bright point indeed when we run out of hearts in Africa that require but lack artificial valves.

Wealth inequalities around the world may be deplorable. But they virtually guarantee growth opportunities for companies that have mastered the risks in slow-growing rich-country markets. They guarantee opportunities to find both unserved customers and more efficient ways to make things. The problem is that doing business in poorer countries is fraught with risk. Part of the risk is dealing with undeveloped and often unenforced commercial codes. But perhaps the larger part of the risk is modifying products and services for radically different wealth profiles and lifestyles.

But what is high risk intelligence in a line of business good for if not tackling risks that could be gateways to growth? In most sectors, players who understand the commercial risks enjoy abundant opportunities to act as transformative agents in emerging markets. There is no need to tolerate low growth in an area where you have high risk intelligence. The opportunities require foreign direct investment. And the investments will be fraught with risk. But *someone* will make that risk profitable.

There are plenty of gaps to fill in the story of risk intelligence. For example, the relevance to a risk of our experience involves its sensitivity to alternative accounts of what drives the risk. Where do those accounts come from? Are they guesses? If so, how could we evaluate the quality of the guesses we make about the risks we face? And what are the implications of risk intelligence for incentive compensation?

But it's already a pretty big story. Like its namesake, emotional intelligence, risk intelligence is about more than an intellectual aptitude.[1] It depends fundamentally on the context of the way we're trying to solve our problems and on our experiential resources for solving them. That context and those resources are basically social. So is risk intelligence.

NOTES

Chapter 1

1. At least, according to one colorful account. David Wallechinsky and Irving Wallace, "Wilmer McLean at the Beginning and End of the War," http://www.trivia-library.com/b/civil-war-history-wilmer-mclean-at-the-beginning-and-end-of-the-war-part-1.htm.

2. "The first battle of the American Civil War, fought in Virginia near Washington, D.C. [and won by the Confederacy]. A year later the Confederacy won another victory near the same place. This battle is called the Second Battle of Bull Run. The South referred to these two encounters as the First and Second Battles of Manassas." E. D. Hirsch Jr., Joseph F. Kett, and James Trefil, eds., *The New Dictionary of Cultural Literacy: What Every American Needs to Know,* 3rd ed. (New York: Houghton Mifflin, 2002).

3. Joe Curreri, "A War Began in His Front Yard—and Ended in His Parlor: The Hidden Face in the Civil War," http://www.historyonline.net/shortstory/ss97-1.htm.

4. Ibid.

5. Paul Milevskiy, Geoffrey C. Kiel, and Gavin J. Nicholson, "Does Board Involvement in Risk Management Add Value?" (Annual Meeting of the Academy of Management: Creating Actionable Knowledge, New Orleans, August 6–11, 2004).

6. Ronald M. Becker, "Lean Manufacturing and the Toyota Production System," http://www.sae.org/topics/leanjun01.htm.

7. Ibid.

8. Careful treatments of how to formulate and select assumptions, hypotheses, or theories are in Joseph M. Firestone and Mark W. McElroy, *Key Issues in the New Knowledge Management* (Boston: Butterworth-Heinemann, 2003), chapter 5; and Ilkka Niiniluoto, *Critical Scientific Realism* (Oxford: Oxford University Press, 1999), chapter 6.

9. Daniel Goleman, *Emotional Intelligence* (New York: Bantam Books, 1995).

Chapter 2

1. Harry Markowitz, "Portfolio Selection," *Journal of Finance,* June 1952.

2. Jeffrey A. Frankel, "Book Review: 'The Crisis of Global Capitalism,' by George Soros," http://ksghome.harvard.edu/~jfrankel/sorosrvw.pdf, 3.

3. William Poole, "Understanding the Term Structure of Interest Rates" (Down Town Association, New York City, June 14, 2005).

4. Benjamin Esty and Pankaj Ghemawat, "Airbus vs. Boeing in Super Jumbos: A Case of Failed Preemption," working paper 02-061, Harvard Business School, Boston, February 2002, 1.

5. Ibid.

6. Ibid., 7.

7. See http://www.boeing.com/companyoffices/aboutus/execprofiles/condit.html.

8. See http://www.airbus.com/en/corporate/people/Forgeard_bio.html.

9. Esty and Ghemawat, "Airbus vs. Boeing in Super Jumbos," 24.

10. Ibid., 31.

11. Ibid., 7.

12. The Group of Thirty introduced the term *value at risk* in 1993, and J.P. Morgan popularized it through its 1994 RiskMetrics risk management service.

13. Martin Christopher and Helen Peck, "The Five Principles of Supply Chain Resilience," *Logistics Europe,* February 2004, 20.

14. See http://www.themoscowtimes.com/stories/2005/01/25/259.html.

15. Christopher and Peck, "The Five Principals of Supply Chain Resilience."

16. AIG, *Annual Report 2003,* 7.

17. Burton G. Malkiel, *A Random Walk Down Wall Street: The Time-Tested Strategy for Successful Investing* (New York: W. W. Norton, 2003), 186–192.

18. Michael E. Porter, *Competitive Strategy: Techniques for Analyzing Industries and Competitors* (New York: Free Press, 1980), 35–36.

19. Ibid., 12.

20. Malkiel, *A Random Walk Down Wall Street,* 245.

21. This is a version of Pascal's wager on the existence of God: better to be wrong six feet under than wrong in eternal damnation. It's from part II, section II of his 1660 *Pensées.* French schoolchildren sometimes learn it as a

play on Henry IV's cynical Catholic conversion to become king: instead of Henry's nonchalant view that *Paris* is worth a *mass,* Pascal argues *mass* is worth a *pari* (or gamble).

22. Karl R. Popper, *The Open Universe* (London: Routledge, 1982).

23. Ibid., 68–77.

24. Ibid., 88.

25. Thomas M. Cover and Joy A. Thomas, *Elements of Information Theory* (New York: Wiley, 1991). See chapter 7 on "Kolmogorov Complexity," 144–145.

26. David S. Landes, *The Wealth and Poverty of Nations: Why Some Are So Rich and Some So Poor* (New York: W. W. Norton, 1998), 295–296.

27. William W. Lewis, *The Power of Productivity: Wealth, Poverty, and the Threat to Global Stability* (Chicago: University of Chicago Press, 2004), 9.

28. William Easterly, *The Elusive Quest for Growth: Economists' Adventures and Misadventures in the Tropics* (Cambridge, MA: MIT Press, 2001).

29. Paul Romer, "The Economics of Growth," *The Concise Encyclopedia of Economics* (http://www.econlib.org/library/Enc/EconomicGrowth.html).

Chapter 3

1. See http://www.nlm.nih.gov/changingthefaceofmedicine/physicians/biography_12.html.

2. The intuition is that just a few major observable risks account for most problematic project situations, much as just a few outcomes in craps—say, 6, 7, and 8—account for a disproportionate number of underlying possible rolls of the dice. This applies Jacob Bernoulli's law of large numbers (*Ars Conjectandi,* 1713), that the average of sufficiently large samples is likely to be arbitrarily close to the population average. Modern information theory formalizes it by defining *typical sets* as samples whose probability is arbitrarily close to the average probability of all possible observations (or, more accurately, the *entropy* of possible observations adjusted for sample size). See Thomas M. Cover and Joy A. Thomas, *Elements of Information Theory* (New York: Wiley, 1991), 50–51.

3. "The Fall of a Corporate Queen," *Economist,* February 5, 2005, 57–58.

4. *Financial Times,* February 1, 2005.

5. Gary Belsky and Thomas Gilovich, *Why Smart People Make Big Money Mistakes and How to Correct Them: Lessons from the New Science of Behavioral Economics* (New York: Simon & Schuster, 2000), chapter 5.

6. Paul Romer, "Beyond the Knowledge Worker," *Worldlink,* January/February 1995.

7. Karl R. Popper, *Objective Knowledge: An Evolutionary Approach*, rev. ed. (New York: Oxford University Press, 1979), 109.

8. Some theorists, like David Miller, prefer to talk about the *corroboration* of hypotheses on the grounds that we always seek greater hypothesis corroboration but we don't necessarily seek high-probability hypotheses. For example, there's nothing necessarily wrong with a zero-probability hypothesis, since it may just make a universal assertion that must be false in most possible states of the world. Reserving the separate concept of corroboration for hypotheses makes it easier to think of *probabilities* as objective and subject to critical evaluation. David Miller, *Critical Rationalism: A Restatement and Defense* (Chicago: Open Court, 1994). Other theorists, like Richard Jeffrey, argue that we *can* apply probabilities to learning about hypotheses and interpret those probabilities as rational subjective degrees of belief. They often look at probability as an extension of logic to sets of alternative hypotheses that meet an exchangeability condition for equal initial plausibility. Richard Jeffrey, *Subjective Probability: The Real Thing* (Cambridge: Cambridge University Press, 2004). Still others play down the conflict, relying on probability to characterize not so much the aims as the methods of critical learning. For example, Ilkka Niiniluoto calls the probability of hypotheses not subjective but epistemic, both useful in accounting for corroboration and yet open to objective critical evaluation. Ilkka Niiniluoto, *Critical Scientific Realism* (Oxford: Oxford University Press, 1999), section 4.5. The present book can't try to resolve the debate but refers neutrally to the changing probability of a hypothesis, given new experience, as a logical device to keep track of the proportion of viable competing hypotheses that experience so far rules out.

9. Karl R. Popper, *Realism and the Aim of Science* (London: Routledge, 1985), 219.

10. See http://www-groups.dcs.st-and.ac.uk/~history/Mathematicians/Shannon.html.

11. C. E. Shannon, "A Mathematical Theory of Communication," *Bell System Technology Journal* 27 (1948): 379–423, 623–656.

12. Myron Tribus, *Thermostatics and Thermodynamics: An Introduction to Energy, Information and States of Matter, with Engineering Applications* (Princeton, NJ: Van Nostrand, 1961).

13. Cover and Thomas, *Elements of Information Theory*, 16–20.

Chapter 4

1. Clayton M. Christensen, *The Innovator's Dilemma: When New Technologies Cause Great Firms to Fail* (Boston: Harvard Business School Press, 1997).

2. This is most true where companies use debt or rely on credit ratings. Since equity investors can diversify risks themselves, they won't necessarily punish a company for more concentrated exposure to a business. But the employees working in that business will feel pressure if there are a lot of ups and downs in their contributions to the firm's overall earnings. In extreme cases, they may seek jobs with competitors whose other businesses better cushion swings in their own results.

3. The Analytic Hierarchy Process implemented in the Expert Choice system is a powerful way to translate subjective rankings into objective priorities or weights. For example, it could produce objective weightings for a list of projects in light of manager ratings of their assessment skills for the various principal project risks they face. T. L. Saaty, *The Analytic Hierarchy Process* (New York: McGraw-Hill, 1980). For information on Expert Choice, refer to http://www.expertchoice.com.

4. Measures for the amount of risk-related experience could be as objective as sales call or supplier review frequencies. Objective measures for the relevance of experiences to a risk include the standard deviation of the likelihood of the experiences, given alternative theories of what drives the risk. Objective measures for the surprise of experiences include estimates of their improbability—for example, the statistical improbability of successful sales conversions. Objective measures for the diversity of experiences include simple counts of unrelated sources.

5. See http://multinationalmonitor.org/mm2004/122004/mokhiber.html.

6. Robert E. Hall, "The Labor Market Is the Key to Understanding the Business Cycle," *National Bureau of Economic Research,* September 23, 2004, http://www.stanford.edu/~rehall.

Chapter 5

1. Is it more accurate to say these risks are *unlearnable* or *truly random*? After all, the most we can often say about a seemingly random process is that a straight description of its results is the simplest way we know to generate, replicate, or learn about it. Information theorists define a set of results as *algorithmically random* if the shortest effectively calculable procedure for generating it (think of a computer program) is as long as the description of the set (see Thomas M. Cover and Joy A. Thomas, *Elements of Information Theory* [New York: Wiley, 1991], 157). This book can treat all unlearnable risks as random since we only need to distinguish them from learnable ones. But there remains an undecided metaphysical question of whether some unlearnable processes are nonrandom.

2. The Sharpe ratio is the ratio of the average return from a risky investment (in excess of the risk-free interest rate) to the volatility of the

investment's returns. Since average returns reflect just the market-related component of total volatility, high Sharpe ratios indicate a high percentage of market-related risk, while low Sharpe ratios indicate a low percentage. This means that projects with high Sharpe ratios should fall to the right of the matrix; those with low Sharpe ratios should fall to the left.

3. The actual number will depend on what level of confidence I require, just as with value at risk. For example, I might want to know the worst case all but 1 percent of the time.

4. Ron Gluckman, http://www.gluckman.com/LaoSilk.html.

5. William Easterly, *The Elusive Quest for Growth: Economists' Adventures and Misadventures in the Tropics* (Cambridge, MA: MIT Press, 2001).

6. Ibid., 275–276.

7. Ibid., 279–280.

8. K. R. Popper, *The Open Society and Its Enemies* (London: Routledge & Kegan Paul, 1945).

Chapter 6

1. Daniel Goleman, *Emotional Intelligence* (New York: Bantam Books, 1995).

INDEX

absolute versus relative cost and risk, 51–53
AIG, 49
Airbus, 38, 39–42, 157
amnesiacs
    described, 86, 91–92
    remedies for record-keeping gaps, 92–93
    risk intelligence pattern, 86, 186
anchoring an experience, 84, 85
Apgar, Virginia
    biographical sketch, 73
    score for newborns, 67
Apple, 132, 134
Armstrong, Michael, 81
AT&T
    cable experience, 79, 81–82
    Internet experience, 80, 81
    risk intelligence score for initiatives, 80
    risk story summary, 82
    wireless experience, 80–81
Australia, 5
automobile manufacturing, 159

banks and risks, 31, 32–36, 116
Battle of Bull Run, 1–3
Bayes, Thomas, 97
BCG growth-share matrix, 129–131
Beane, Billy, 66, 67
Belsky, Gary, 84

Bernanke, Ben, 36
Boeing, 38, 39–42, 157
Boston Consulting Group, 129–131
Bradley debt relief plan, 166
business cycle and risk strategies, 140–142

Car Talk (radio show), 101
Cassidy, Carol, 169–170
CFOs and risk strategy audits, 128
China, 49, 139, 178
Christensen, Clayton, 111
classic borrowers, 153–154
competitive advantage and risk. See risk-based competitive advantage
Competitive Strategy (Porter), 51–52, 53
concavity of market values, 176
Condit, Phil, 38, 40
conditional entropy, 102
controllers and risk strategy audits, 128
COSO framework, 127
customers and market feedback, 173–174
customer umbrellas, 150, 152–157

discontinuous innovation, 111–112
diversifiability and risk, 146–147, 149, 151–152

205

diversification, unprincipled, 139
Dizard, Stephen, 167

Easterly, William, 178
ecologies, risk
    market fragmentation and, 179
    networks for risk management
        and, 145–147
economic development
    ethnic fragmentation and, 179
    impact of fragmentation on,
        179–180, 197
    incubator markets and, 177–179
Elusive Quest for Growth, The
    (Easterly), 178
emerging-market risk, 168–171, 180
encyclopedists
    described, 86, 88–89
    improbability gap, 89
    record keeping and, 91
    remedies for improbability gaps,
        89–91
    risk intelligence pattern, 88, 186
entropy and experience, 102
Ericsson, 45, 47–49
ethnic fragmentation and economic
    development, 179
European Union, 180–181

fall strategies, 137–139
feedback, market, 175–178,
    195–196
fish market, central Tokyo, 9–10
flat-field risks
    benefits of, 164–166
    example of, 166–168
    randomness and, 163–164
Ford Motor Company, 6
foreign direct investors and risk
    networks, 172–173
Forgeard, Noël, 38, 40
fragmentation, market, 179–180

Gaskell, Neil, 171
General Motors, 9, 138
Gerstner, Lou, 155

Gilovich, Thomas, 84
Gramm-Leach-Bliley Act, 36
Greenspan, Alan, 36
Grove, Andy, 56
growth-share matrix, BCG, 129–131

Harry Potter (Rowling), 84
high-road risk-role migration,
    160–161
hiring risk example, 46–47
housing market risk example, 43–44

IBM, 17, 155
impressionists
    anchoring and improbability of
        key experiences, 83–84
    relevance gaps, 84–86
    remedies for relevance gaps, 87–88
    risk intelligence pattern, 86–87, 186
incubator markets, 177–179
India, 178
information technology teams and
    risk strategy audits, 126
Innovator's Dilemma, The
    (Christensen), 111
insurance sales territories and
    customer feedback, 175–177
interest rates and learnable risks,
    32–36
Internet-related strategic risks, 159

Japan and traditional risk
    assessment, 9–10

Kahneman, Daniel, 84
kanban cards, 7, 10
Kodak, 129

Lao Textiles, 169–170
law of risk gravity, 109
learnable risks
    accuracy of worst-case loss
        estimates and, 49–50
    assessing versus managing, 30–31
    avoiding under- or overestimating
        risk, 49

challenges arising from, 27–30
competitive advantage and (*see* risk-based competitive advantage)
cost of poor assessment skills in managing, 39–42
defined, 25, 26–27
enterprise risk management and, 23–25
hiring uncertainty example, 46–47
importance of risk assessment skills in managing, 31, 36–38
interest rates and, 32–36
random risks contrasted with, 46–47
random risks defined, 25–27
risk factor analysis and, 42–45
steps for improving management of, 184–185, 194–195
legal and audit teams and risk strategy audits, 128
Lehman Brothers, 119, 120
Lewis, Michael, 66
low-road risk-role migration, 160

Malkiel, Burton, 55, 58
market intensity measurement, 147, 149, 151–152
matrix, risk strategy. *See* risk strategy matrixes
Matsushita, 134
McLean, Wilmer, 1–3, 21
measuring risk intelligence. *See* risk IQ
Mexico, 166–168
Microsoft, 132
Moneyball (Lewis), 66
myths about risk
no pattern to risk development, 16–18
no persistent winners and losers, 15–16
randomness of all risks, 14
same results no matter who bears risk, 18–20

Nestlé, 135
networks for risk management
concavity of market values and, 176
critical role of customer and market feedback, 173–174
diversifiability of risks and, 146–147, 149, 151–152
drivers of the value of market feedback, 175–176
emerging-market risk and, 168–171, 180
financial structure implications of focusing and dabbling, 161–162
flat-field risk advantages, 164–166
flat-field risk and debt relief, 166–168
flat-field risks and randomness, 163–164
foreign direct investors and, 172–173
gauging coherence and relevance of feedback, 176–178
high-road risk-role migration, 160–161
incubator markets and, 177–179
low-road risk-role migration, 160
market fragmentation and economic development, 179–180
market intensity of risks and, 147, 149, 151–152
project risk migration and, 158–159
risk ecologies and, 145–147
risk intelligence and, 18–20
risk-role factors, 145–146
risk-role matrix (*see* risk-role matrix)
risk roles in foreign direct investment, 169–172
Nokia, 45, 47–49

Ollila, Jorma, 48
Open Society and Its Enemies, The (Popper), 180

Open Universe, The (Popper), 57
operations teams and risk strategy
    audits, 126
outsourcing, 168

Pareto, Vilfredo, 72
Pareto analysis, 75
People's Insurance Company of
    China (PICC), 49
Pfizer, 119–121, 138
pipelines, risk
    concept of, 18, 113–115
    risk strategy audit and, 106–107
    steps for improving risk IQ using,
        189–190
Poole, William, 36
Popper, Karl, 57, 92, 180
Porter, Michael, 51–52, 53
procurement officers and risk
    strategy audits, 127–128

quality control leaders and risk
    strategy audits, 127

random risks
    complexity and, 58
    defined, 25–27
    enterprise risk management and,
        23–25
    flat-field risks and, 163–164
    learnable risks contrasted with,
        46–47
    risk-based competitive advantage
        and, 54–56
    role of self-reference in
        randomness, 57–58
random walk theory, 57–58
rates of return for investors, 155
real estate and risk intelligence,
    68–71
relevance
    complementary roles of surprise
        and, 96–97, 98–99, 100–103
    as a component of the value of an
        experience, 100–103
    of feedback, 176–178
    gaps and impressionists, 84–88

measure of, 102
    of a typical experience, 74–75
research and development teams and
    risk strategy audits, 128
risk assessment patterns
    amnesiacs, 86, 91–93, 186
    encyclopedists, 86, 88–91, 186
    impressionists, 83–88, 186
risk-based competitive advantage
    absolute versus relative cost and,
        51–53
    complexity of processes and, 58
    cost of handling risk and,
        59–61
    persistent differences in risk factor
        assumptions and, 50–51
    random risk and, 54–56
    risk assessment superiority and,
        45, 47–49
    source in risk assessment skills
        advantages, 42–43, 53–54
    why arising now, 59–61
risk distributors, 157–158
risk ecologies
    market fragmentation and, 179
    networks for risk management
        and, 145–147
risk gravity, law of, 109
risk intelligence
    comparative gap in risk
        assessment skills and, 6
    core competencies and, 21
    described, 3, 12–13, 21
    Japanese examples of, 7–11
    learnable risks and, 14–16
    learning gaps and, 11–12
    life cycle of projects risks and,
        16–18
    measuring (*see* risk IQ)
    networks of partners and, 18–20
        (*see also* networks for risk
        management)
    Pareto analysis and, 75
    pipelines of risky projects and, 18
    risk selection and, 4–6
    rules of, 13–20
    scores (*see* risk IQ)

steps for improving (*see* steps for
improving risk intelligence)
types of risk subject to, 12
risk IQ (risk intelligence score)
case example (*see* AT&T)
complementary roles of relevance
and surprise, 96–97, 98–99,
100–103
diversity of experiences
comparison, 78
frequency of related experiences,
74
importance of risk assessment
skills, 64–67
improving scores, 186–187
managing the stages of assessment
skills, 93–94
next steps after scoring, 71–72
patterns of risk assessment skills,
93–94 (*see also* amnesiacs;
encyclopedists; impressionists)
probabilistic inference and risk
assessment, 97–98
record keeping, 78
relevance, measure of, 102
relevance as a component of the
value of an experience, 100–103
(*see also* surprise)
relevance of a typical experience,
74–76
risk selection and, 72, 74–79
scoring illustration, 68–71
Shannon information and,
100–101
surprise, memorability, or
improbability of typical
experience, 76–78
surprise or improbability as a
component of the value of an
experience, 100–103
team building and, 95–96
value of information, 94
risk pipelines
concept of, 18, 113–115
risk strategy audit and, 106–107
steps for improving risky project
results using, 189–190

risk-role matrix
classic borrowers, 153–154
customer umbrellas, 150, 152–153
described, 144, 147–150
risk distributors, 157–158
shock absorbers, 154–157
steps for improving risky project
results using, 191–194
risk strategy audit
acquisition planning application
of, 139
BCG growth-share matrix and,
129–131
business cycle and, 140–142
competitive threats revealed by,
110–112
corporate applications of, 126–128
discontinuous innovation and,
111–112
inputs template, 124
pipelines of risky projects revealed
by, 106–107, 113–115
portfolio view illustration, 125
precision of, 125
project size inputs to, 123
reap-and-sow versus nurture
strategies, 132
risk concentrations revealed by,
109–110
risk diversification inputs to,
124–125
risk intelligence inputs to, 122
risk portfolios and, 106
risk strategy matrixes resulting
from, 117–121, 129–130
risk strategy patterns and
weaknesses, 132–138
steps for improving risk IQ using,
187–189
subjectivity in, 121, 123
trade-offs in risk strategies
revealed by, 115–117
unprincipled diversification and,
139
risk strategy matrixes
case examples, 119–121
described, 117–118

risk strategy matrixes (*continued*)
  growth-share matrixes and,
    129–130
  life cycle of risks and, 118–119
risk strategy patterns
  fall, 137–138
  overview, 132
  spring, 134–136
  summer, 136–137
  winter, 133–134
Romer, Paul, 60, 92
Rowling, J. K., 84
rules of risk
  identifying learnable risks, 14
  selecting learnable risks, 15–16
  sequencing learnable risks in a
    pipeline, 16–18
  using risk networks, 18–20

sales and marketing teams and risk
    strategy audits, 126
Sarbanes-Oxley, 127
scoring risk intelligence. *See* risk IQ
Shannon, Claude, 100
Sharpe ratio, 152, 192
Shell Oil, 171
shock absorbers, 154–157
software versus wetware, 92
solutions businesses, 155–156
Sony Corporation, 134
Soros, George, 28
spring strategies, 134–136
steps for improving risk intelligence
  aligning risk selection with orga-
    nizational structure, 193–194
  allocating roles in risk partner
    networks, 191–193
  auditing risk strategies, 187–189
  balancing risk and growth,
    196–197

classifying risk strategies and
    pipelines, 189–190
  ensuring relevant customer
    feedback, 195–196
  identifying learnable risks, 184–185
  improving risk intelligence scores,
    186–187
  scoring risk IQ, 185, 186
  transforming learnable risks into
    flat-field risks, 194–195
summer strategies, 136–137
surprisal of a piece of information,
    100
surprise
  complementary roles of relevance
    and, 96–97, 98–99, 100–103
  memorability or improbability of
    typical experience and, 75–77,
    100–103

teams and risk intelligence, 95–96,
    126
Toyota, 6, 7, 8–9
treasurers and risk strategy audits,
    128
Tsukiji Market, 9–10
tsunami, Indian Ocean, 26–27
Tversky, Amos, 84

University of Queensland, 5
unprincipled diversification, 139

value at risk, 44–45, 94

Wal-Mart Stores, 136, 157
wetware versus software, 92
Williams Companies, 65–66
winter strategies, 133–134

yield curve, 32–36

ABOUT THE AUTHOR

David Apgar is a managing director at the Corporate Executive Board, whose best-practices research programs for corporate controllers and treasurers he launched between 2001 and 2003. He joined the Board in 1998 from McKinsey, where he served insurance, reinsurance, and capital markets clients as a consultant and an engagement manager for three years. Prior to that, David was responsible for numerous finance company, bank, and insurer M&A assignments as a vice president in Lehman Brothers' Financial Institutions Group, and for building a framework for bank security sales as Senior Policy Adviser to the Comptroller of the Currency. He proposed a debt relief program for Mexico and designed the precursor to interest rate relief Brady bonds as staff economist to Senator Bill Bradley.

David holds an AB from Harvard, an MA from Oxford, and a PhD from the Rand Graduate School.